ADULTING MADE SIMPLE

ESSENTIAL LIFE SKILLS FOR YOUNG ADULTS

EVERYTHING YOU NEED TO KNOW TO LIVE INDEPENDENTLY, BUILD WEALTH, STRONG RELATIONSHIPS, A DREAM CAREER, AND LIVE YOUR BEST LIFE!

LOREN HAYES

© **Copyright 2025 - All rights reserved.**

The content contained within this book may not be reproduced, duplicated, or transmitted without direct written permission from the author or the publisher.

Under no circumstances will any blame or legal responsibility be held against the publisher, or author, for any damages, reparation, or monetary loss due to the information contained within this book, either directly or indirectly.

Legal Notice:

This book is copyright protected. It is only for personal use. You cannot amend, distribute, sell, use, quote, or paraphrase any part, or the content within this book, without the author or publisher's permission.

Disclaimer Notice:

Please note that the information contained within this document is for educational and entertainment purposes only. All effort has been executed to present accurate, up-to-date, reliable, complete information. No warranties of any kind are declared or implied. Readers acknowledge that the author is not rendering legal, financial, medical, or professional advice. The content within this book has been derived from various sources. Please consult a licensed professional before attempting any techniques outlined in this book.

By reading this document, the reader agrees that under no circumstances is the author responsible for any losses, direct or indirect, that are incurred due to the use of the information in this document, including, but not limited to, errors, omissions, or inaccuracies.

CONTENTS

Introduction   7

1. FINANCIAL LITERACY FOR THE FUTURE   9
   Why Financial Literacy Matters   10
   Opening Your First Bank Account and Paying Bills Like a Pro   11
   How to Build a Budget that Works (and Doesn't Feel Like a Punishment)   12
   Understanding Credit and Managing Debt (yup, it's a thing)   14
   The Secret to Building Wealth   16
   Filing Your Taxes (it's not as scary as you think!)   17
   Action Plan   19

2. COOKING BASICS AND MEAL PLANNING FOR BEGINNERS   21
   Why Learn to Cook?: Save Money, Eat Better, Impress Everyone   21
   Basic Cooking Techniques   23
   Cooking Hacks: Shortcuts to Delicious and Stress-Free Meals   25
   Kitchen Essentials: Must-Have Tools for Every Home Cook   26
   Healthy Eating Made Easy   27
   Quick and Easy Meal Ideas   28
   Meal Planning Like a Pro: Stay Organized, Save Time, Eat Better   30
   Smart Grocery Shopping: Strategies to Save Money and Avoid Waste   31
   Your First Meal Plan: A Sample Menu and Shopping List to Get Started   32
   Action Plan   34

3. HEALTH, HYGIENE, AND WELLNESS FUNDAMENTALS   37
   Personal Hygiene Essentials: Stay Fresh, Stay Confident   37
   Fuel Your Body Right: Simple and Smart Healthy Eating Habits   39

Move It to Improve It: Physical Activity for Energy and Strength	41
Mind Over Matter: Managing Stress, Anxiety, and Emotional Wellness	42
Navigating Doctors and Medical Care: What You Need to Know	45
Action Plan	46
4. TIME MANAGEMENT AND MAXIMIZING PRODUCTIVITY	**49**
Mastering Time Management	49
Mastering Organization: Hacks, Apps, and Tools for a Productive Life	52
Goal Setting and Achievement	55
Multitasking: The Good and the Bad	56
Action Plan	58
5. CAREER PLANNING AND JOB SKILLS	**61**
From Search to Success: Nail Your Job Hunt	61
Crafting Your Resume: Selling Yourself	62
Ace Your Job Interview	66
Networking and Building Relationships	67
Workplace Etiquette	68
Excelling in Your Job	70
Action Plan	71
Make a Difference with Your Review	75
6. COMMUNICATION, SOCIAL SKILLS, AND RELATIONSHIP BUILDING	**77**
Effective Communication: Talking the Talk	77
Making Friends and Building Relationships	79
Conflict Resolution: Avoiding Drama	81
Manners Matter: Etiquette for Common Social Situations	83
Action Plan	86
7. DIGITAL LITERACY AND ONLINE SAFETY	**89**
Managing Your Social Media Presence: Curating Your Online Brand	89
Recognizing and Avoiding Online Threats: Staying Safe Online	91
Don't Be *That* Person: Mastering Online Etiquette	93
Online Dating Safety	94

Your Online Actions Matter: Be a Responsible Digital
Citizen   95
Action Plan   97

8. RENTING 101   101
Finding Your Perfect Pad   101
Understanding Lease Agreements. Read before you sign   103
Roommate Agreements: Setting Boundaries and
Expectations   104
Moving In and Out   105
Being a Good Tenant   107
Don't Get Caught Off Guard: Protect Your Belongings
& Know Your Rights   108
Action Plan   109

9. HOUSEHOLD MANAGEMENT MASTERY   111
Cleaning and Maintenance: Keeping Your Space Tidy
with Minimal Effort   112
Laundry 101   114
Home Safety Tips: Preventing and Handling
Emergencies   116
Basic Home Repairs   117
Understanding Utilities: Managing Bills and
Energy Use   119
Action Plan   120

10. BUYING AND MAINTAINING A CAR   123
Freedom on Wheels: Weighing the Pros and Cons of
Car Ownership   123
Finding Your Perfect Ride   124
Paying for Your Ride   125
Protecting Your Investment   127
Keeping Your Ride in Tip-Top Shape   128
Driving Responsibly   130
Action Plan   131

You've Got This!   133
References   135

INTRODUCTION

MASTERING ADULTING WITHOUT THE STRESS

Why These Skills Matter

Let's be honest —adulting can feel like a never-ending to-do list. But knowing how to manage your money, cook a decent meal, stay on top of responsibilities, and handle social situations makes life way less stressful. Plus, being self-sufficient gives you more freedom—no more panicked calls to your parents or Googling "how to fix a flat tire" from the side of the road. Here's why these skills are total game-changers:

- **Financial Independence = More Choice.** Understanding budgeting, credit, and debt keeps you from constantly worrying about money and helps you build a future where you can afford the fun stuff, too.
- **Self-Sufficiency = Greater Confidence.** Cooking, cleaning, and basic car maintenance mean you won't have to live off instant ramen or freak out when your check engine light comes on.
- **Career Skills = Bigger Paychecks.** Mastering job hunting, interviews, and workplace etiquette helps you land better opportunities, score your dream job, and get ahead faster.

- **Time Management Skills = More Freedom.** Learning to prioritize tasks, stay organized, and set goals allows you to get more done in less time, leaving you with extra hours to enjoy the things you love and focus on what truly matters.
- **Social Smarts = Stronger Relationships.** Good communication makes it easier to make friends, navigate conflicts, and build connections that matter.
- **Healthy Habits = Less Stress.** Taking care of your physical and mental health means less stress, better focus, and more energy to go after your goals.
- **Smart Decisions = Fewer Regrets.** Whether it's signing a lease, choosing insurance, or staying safe online, knowing how to make informed choices saves you from costly mistakes.

Adulting Isn't About Perfection—It's About Progress

No one expects you to have it all figured out overnight. The goal isn't perfection—it's confidence in handling real-life situations. Each chapter in this book breaks things down into simple, practical steps—no complicated jargon, just real advice you can actually use. Think of it as your go-to guide for thriving on your own.

By the time you finish this book, you'll know how to manage your money, cook meals that don't suck, keep your space in order, land (and keep) a job, and so much more. And the best part? Once you master these skills, you'll have more time and freedom to focus on what really matters—building the life you want, on your terms.

So, ready to level up your adulting game? Let's get started!

1

FINANCIAL LITERACY FOR THE FUTURE

It's the end of the month, and you're staring at your bank balance with confusion and dread. Where did all your money go? You were pretty sure you'd been careful, yet somehow, your funds vanished faster than your motivation to clean your room. Sound familiar? You're not alone. For many people, managing money feels like trying to solve a Rubik's Cube in the dark.

But here's the good news: financial literacy is your flashlight. It's the skill set that turns the chaos of adulting into something manageable—even empowering. Financial literacy is all about understanding how money works. It's the ability to budget, save, invest, and make smart financial decisions. Think of it as learning a new language—one you'll use every day of your life.

And here's the best part: becoming fluent in this language can change everything. Imagine never panicking over a bill again, confidently saving for your dream trip, or feeling in control of your financial future. Financial literacy doesn't just help you survive—it helps you thrive. It opens doors, creates opportunities, and, most importantly, gives you the freedom to make choices, pursue your dreams, and live life on your own terms.

In this section, we'll break it down step by step: how to budget without stress, build savings effortlessly, and even start investing for your future. Ready? Let's turn on the flashlight and get started.

WHY FINANCIAL LITERACY MATTERS

Let's get real for a second—money impacts everything you do. Your financial situation shapes your life, from where you live to what you eat, and even how you spend your downtime. It's not just about paying bills or saving up for that concert ticket; it's about having the freedom to make choices that lead to an awesome future. When you understand how to manage your money, you gain control over your life. You start avoiding the stress of piling up debt, and suddenly, bills become less of a burden and more of a routine part of life. This understanding helps you become proactive rather than reactive. You stop playing catch-up and start planning ahead.

Being financially literate is like having a superpower. It means you can confidently navigate the financial world, making decisions that are right for you. You know how to budget, so you're not blindsided by unexpected expenses. You understand savings and investments, so your money works for you, not vice versa. And when it comes to credit, you're the one in charge, not the lender. Financial literacy turns money from a source of stress into a tool you can use to achieve your goals. Whether it's buying a car, moving out on your own, or even just treating yourself to a night out with friends, knowing how to handle your finances makes it all possible.

Financial literacy matters because it equips you with the necessary tools to succeed. It's not about being rich; it's about being smart with what you have. It's about making informed decisions, feeling secure in your future, and having the confidence to pursue your dreams. Financial literacy is the foundation for a life of independence and success. So, while it might seem boring or complicated initially, remember: every skill you learn today is a step toward the future you want. And that's worth every penny.

OPENING YOUR FIRST BANK ACCOUNT AND PAYING BILLS LIKE A PRO

Opening your first bank account is a big step toward adulthood, blending freedom with responsibility. Choosing the right account is simpler than it seems. Think of a **checking account** as your everyday wallet—where your paycheck lands and where you handle daily expenses like groceries and Netflix subscriptions. Meanwhile, a **savings account** is your piggy bank, where you stash away money for future adventures or unexpected surprises, earning a bit of interest as a bonus. Checking accounts offer conveniences like **online bill payments** and **overdraft protection**, which covers transactions when you spend more than you have in your account, usually for a steep fee. In contrast, savings accounts encourage long-term goals by keeping your funds out of easy reach, making it less tempting to dip into your savings for unnecessary splurges.

Consider whether an online or traditional bank fits your lifestyle as you weigh your options. **Online banks** often boast fewer fees and higher interest rates, which is ideal if you're all about digital convenience. However, **traditional banks** might offer more branches and ATMs, making them handy if you prefer in-person services or need to deposit cash regularly. Also, watch for sneaky fees—some banks might charge you for things like having a low balance or using an out-of-network ATM. It's wise to pick a bank that won't nibble away at your savings with these hidden charges. NerdWallet suggests options like Ally Bank, known for its no overdraft fees and extensive ATM network, or Discover Bank, celebrated for its no monthly fees and impressive online experience. Once you've chosen a bank, opening an account is simple. You'll just need your ID, proof of address, and Social Security Number. It's a good idea to set up checking and savings accounts to keep your finances organized.

Your checking account will come with a **debit card**, which acts like cash but offers more convenience. Use it wisely by staying aware of your account balance and opting for overdraft protection only as a last resort. Make sure to keep your card secure by never sharing your PIN and being cautious when shopping online. Always look for "https" in the website's URL to confirm it's a safe place to enter your information. Use **mobile wallets** like Apple Pay or Google Pay for added security and convenience, so you don't always have to carry cash.

Paying bills might seem like a hassle, but with some simple organization, it can be effortless. Using your checking account's Bill Pay feature, consider setting up **automatic payments** for recurring expenses like rent and your phone bill—this way, you'll never miss a deadline. Check your account balance frequently to avoid overdrafts and the fees that come with them.

Online and **mobile banking** will be your go-to tools. They let you monitor your spending, transfer funds, and pay bills from anywhere, making it feel like you have a personal banker in your pocket.

Building solid banking habits now will pay off in the long run. Check your account weekly to catch any unauthorized charges or errors, and set reminders for bill due dates or set up automatic bill pay. Avoid relying on overdraft protection like a financial safety net. Take these steps now, and you'll be well on your way to handling your finances like a pro.

HOW TO BUILD A BUDGET THAT WORKS (AND DOESN'T FEEL LIKE A PUNISHMENT)

Budgeting might sound about as fun as getting a tooth pulled but think of it more like plotting out an epic road trip. You wouldn't just hop in your car and drive aimlessly, hoping to stumble upon your destination. Instead, you'd map out your route, plan some pit stops, and maybe even budget for a few spontaneous adventures along the way. That's exactly how **budgeting** works for your money. It's about knowing where your cash comes from and where it goes. Picture your **income** as the fuel for your financial journey, whether it's from your part-time gig, allowance, or that side hustle. Then there are **fixed expenses**—the non-negotiable stops on your map, like rent, car insurance, and your phone bill, which show up like clockwork every month. **Variable expenses**, on the other hand, are those detours and scenic routes you didn't quite plan for, like grabbing dinner with friends or splurging on a new game. Keeping an eye on these helps you avoid running out of gas—or cash—in the middle of nowhere.

Setting **financial goals** is like mapping out your journey. **Short-term goals** are like quick trips to the next town—maybe saving up for those concert tickets or a new pair of kicks. **Long-term goals** require a bit more strategy, like building up savings for a car or a house, grad school, or an emergency fund for unexpected expenses. The key is to prioritize needs over wants. Make sure the essentials—like rent and groceries—are covered before indulging in the extras. It's all about balance; you shouldn't feel like you're missing out, but you also don't want to find yourself scrambling to pay the bills.

Okay, let's break it down step-by-step. First, jot down every source of **income** you have. Next, divide your **expenses** into two categories: **needs and wants**. Here's a straightforward strategy to manage your finances—the **50/30/20 rule**. Allocate 50% of your income to cover essential needs, 30% for your wants, and 20% for savings. Your budget will look different based on your situation. For example, if you're a student living at home with a part-time job, you might have more funds for wants vs. someone renting an apartment and paying for a car, or you may be aggressively saving for a car and allocating more than 20%. It's important to **track your spending** for a month to see where your money goes. Use apps like NerdWallet or good old Google Sheets to keep tabs on everything, or look at your last month's checking statement to see all your transactions. Reflect on last month's expenses: did you meet your needs? Did you go overboard on wants? Were you able to save anything? If not, why?

Budgeting 50/30/20 Rule

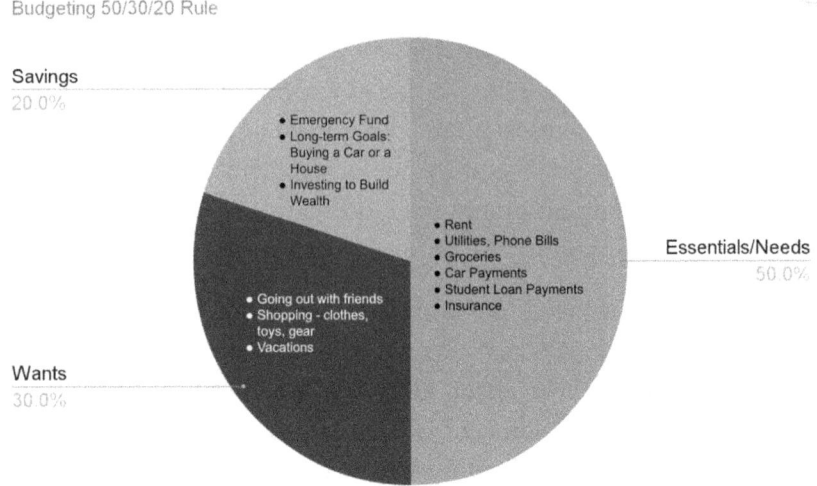

Budgeting isn't a one-and-done deal; it's an ongoing process. Life throws curveballs, like unexpected car repairs or holiday shopping sprees. **Adjusting your budget** to handle these surprises is key. **Control your variable spending**—think cooking at home instead of dining out, or maybe cutting that Netflix subscription for a bit. Sometimes, bigger lifestyle changes are necessary—like using public transport instead of Uber, sharing an apartment to cut rent, or switching to a cheaper phone plan. **Check in regularly** to make sure you're on track and tweak as needed. Remember, the goal is to create a budget that works for you, not against you. So, go ahead and map out your financial road trip—it's a journey worth taking.

UNDERSTANDING CREDIT AND MANAGING DEBT (YUP, IT'S A THING)

Credit and debt might seem like two sides of the same coin, but they play totally different roles in your financial story. Think of **credit** as a financial tool—it lets you borrow cash or buy things now with the promise to pay later. When used wisely, it can help you get better interest rates, secure loans, get approved for apartments, or even land certain jobs. But then there's the downside: debt. **Debt** is what you owe, usually with interest added, and if you don't keep it under control, it can become a major weight holding you back. Imagine using a credit card to buy a $100 pair of sneakers at a 20% interest rate and only making the minimum payments. In two years, those sneakers could cost you $134. Now picture that happening with every splurge—debt can add up quickly and spiral out of control. If you can't afford to pay it off in full right away, it'll only get harder to tackle the larger amount as interest adds up over time.

Not all debt is created equal, though. Some debt, like student loans or a mortgage, can be an investment in your future, helping you build a stable life. These are often considered '**good debt**' because they typically come with lower interest rates and can lead to increased earning potential or home equity. On the other hand, '**bad debt**'—think high-interest credit card balances—can drain your finances and cause stress. It's crucial to consider **interest rates** when borrowing; they determine how much extra you'll pay over time.

Let's compare $500 in credit card debt versus $500 in a savings account to see how interest works in opposite ways: With $500 in credit card debt at 20% interest, you'll owe around $600 after one year if you don't pay it off—an extra $100 in interest. In contrast, $500 in a savings account at 2% interest only earns about $10 in a year. **Debt grows much faster than savings**, making it crucial to avoid high-interest debt whenever possible. That's why prevention is key. Budget wisely and avoid unnecessary spending. If you can't pay for something in full, ask yourself if it's truly a need or just a want.

Building credit means showing lenders you're reliable by borrowing and repaying money responsibly. Building a strong credit foundation starts with understanding your **credit score**—a measure of your creditworthiness. It's a three-digit number that lenders use to decide whether to offer you credit and on what terms. It can even impact rental applications and job offers. Credit scores range from poor to excellent, with good scores typically starting around 670. You can get a **free credit report** from annualcreditreport.com annually to check your score and see what's affecting it. The most important things you can do to improve your score are to pay bills on time, keep credit card balances low, and avoid frequent new credit applications.

One way to build credit without getting into debt is by using **secured credit cards**. These cards require a cash deposit upfront, which becomes your credit limit. It's a safe way to build credit because it limits your spending to your deposit. Look for cards with no fees, like those offered by Capital One or Bank of America. When managing credit cards, remember they are not free money. Use them for emergencies, and pay your balance in full each month to avoid interest charges. Never charge more than you can pay off in a few months.

THE SECRET TO BUILDING WEALTH

Imagine planting a tiny seed today that grows into a mighty tree over the years. That's what starting to **save early** does for your finances. The magic ingredient here is **compound interest**—essentially, it's interest on your interest, which means your money doesn't just add up; it multiplies over time. Let's look at a dramatic comparison to highlight the power of compound interest: imagine two friends, Alex and Jordan. Alex invests $5,000/year from ages 20 to 30 (a total of $50,000 in 10 years) and stops. Jordan invests $5,000/year from ages 30 to 60 (a total of $150,000 in 30 years). Both accounts earn an average of 7% annual interest. By age 60, Alex has $602,070, while Jordan has $540,741. Despite contributing $100,000 less, Alex ends up with more because starting early allows compound interest to grow exponentially over time. It's like a snowball effect, where even small, consistent savings can turn into a substantial amount over the years. But remember, this principle applies to debt as well. Unpaid debt can grow just as fast, turning manageable amounts into financial burdens if not addressed.

Saving smartly means considering **opportunity costs**—the value of what you give up when you choose one option over another. For example, imagine you spend $50/week on clothes or video games.

That's $200 a month or $2,400 a year. If you saved that money instead and put it into an account earning 5% annual interest, in three years, you'd have over $7,500. In five years, it would grow to over $13,000. $50 doesn't seem like much, but $7,500 is a lot! And that's all from multiple decisions involving small amounts: small amounts add up to big savings over time. So, ask yourself, "Do I really need this now, or could it grow into something more?" This **mindset shift** can help you see spending differently. Prioritize **paying yourself first**—after covering essentials, always set aside a portion of your income for savings. A guideline like the 50/30/20 rule helps, and many banks offer tools like **round-up savings** or **automatic transfers** to help make saving even easier.

Once you've got some savings, it's time to think about **investing**. Start with a **savings account** for **short-term needs** or emergencies. For **medium-term goals**, look into **Certificates of Deposit (CDs) or money market accounts**, which offer higher interest rates without the risks of stocks. When you're ready for the **long haul** and have a solid financial base, consider diving into **stocks, bonds, mutual funds, or exchange-traded funds (ETFs)** for wealth accumulation. Real estate could also be an option down the line. The idea is to diversify—spread your investments around so you're not relying on just one source of growth. In the early stages, focus on building an emergency fund through a savings account. As your savings grow and you're sure you won't need that money for a while, consider higher fixed-interest investments. When you've accumulated at least $1,000 and can resist the urge to dip into your savings, then you can explore stock market investing and retirement savings.

FILING YOUR TAXES (IT'S NOT AS SCARY AS YOU THINK!)

Alright, let's tackle taxes. The word alone can make your eyes glaze over, but it's not as complicated as it sounds. **Taxes** are payments you contribute to keep things running—like roads, schools, and emergency services. When you get your paycheck, you'll notice deductions labeled as Social Security and Medicare taxes. These are automatically taken out and help fund important programs for retirees and those with disabilities. On top of those, there are the federal and state income taxes. These depend on how much you earn. If you've made over a certain threshold—say, around $14,600 in 2024—you'll need to file a tax return. Not sure if you're required to file? The IRS has a handy tool online called the Interactive Tax Assistant https://www.irs.gov/help/ita that can guide you through the process.

If you need to file, circle **April 15th** on your calendar, the typical deadline for submitting your tax return. However, the date can shift if it falls on a weekend or holiday. Filing taxes might seem daunting, but it's very doable on your own, especially if your financial situation isn't too complex. First, gather the necessary documents like your **W-2** from any employer or **1099** forms if you earned freelance income or from your investment accounts. You might wonder whether you should file taxes yourself or hire a tax professional. For most young adults, **tax software** is the way to go. It's straightforward, cost-effective, and offers an invaluable learning experience for the future. Programs like **TurboTax** guide you through the process step-by-step, ensuring you don't miss any crucial deductions or credits.

If your taxes are more complicated—like if you run a business, earn a lot of self-employment income, or have a bunch of deductions (expenses that reduce the amount of income you're taxed on)—it might be worth seeing a tax pro. This isn't common for most young adults, but if it applies to you, a professional can handle the tricky details and give personalized advice. For most straightforward situations, though, tax software is an easy and affordable way to file.

So there you have it. Filing taxes is a part of adulting that might seem intimidating at first, but with a bit of preparation and the right tools, it becomes just another task to check off your list. Whether you're looking forward to a sweet refund or just want to ensure you're complying with the law, understanding taxes is crucial. It's about taking charge of another aspect of your financial life, setting you up for success and independence. And who knows? You might even be satisfied knowing you've nailed another adult responsibility.

ACTION PLAN

1. **Open bank accounts:**
    - Open a checking and savings account.
    - Obtain a debit card and set up your PIN.
    - Set up online banking on your laptop or mobile banking on your smartphone.
    - Set up automated savings and start early: Direct deposit from your job or recurring transfers into your savings account. The sooner you start saving, the more time your money has to grow.

2. **Automate Finances:**
    - Set up automated online bill pay for recurring expenses like phone bills and rent.
    - If you've saved over $1,000, explore medium-term investments like CDs to grow your savings.

3. **Create and Adjust Your Budget**:
    - Use the **50/30/20 rule**: 50% for needs, 30% for wants, and 20% for savings.
    - Identify short-term and long-term financial goals with target amounts.
    - Set up a budget tracker using apps like NerdWallet or Google Sheets.
    - Review last month's expenses and adjust your spending to ensure you save at least 20% monthly for emergencies and irregular expenses.

- **Save often**: Make saving a regular habit, even if it's just small amounts—consistency matters more than size.

4. **Master your credit**:
    - Request your free credit report, correct errors, and work to improve your score if it's below 670.
    - If you have credit card debt, stop using the card or cancel it to avoid accumulating more debt. Create an aggressive savings plan to pay it off immediately.
    - Open a secured credit card to build credit responsibly. Deposit an amount equal to your 30% "wants" budget and pay it off completely every month.

5. **Prepare for Taxes**:
    - Determine whether you need to file taxes this year.
    - In February or March, gather W2s, 1099s, and other tax documents and store them together in a safe place.
    - Set up a TurboTax account and prepare to file your taxes by April 15.

2

COOKING BASICS AND MEAL PLANNING FOR BEGINNERS

Picture this: it's a lazy Sunday morning, and your stomach growls like a bear waking from hibernation. You could grab some cereal or order from your favorite diner, but what if you could whip up a delicious breakfast that's satisfying and easy on the wallet? Learning to cook is like unlocking a secret level in the game of life. Not only do you save money by avoiding the takeout trap, but you also gain the power of knowing what goes into your meals. Plus, nothing boosts your confidence like serving up a meal you've crafted from scratch—whether it's impressing your friends, family, or someone special.

WHY LEARN TO COOK?: SAVE MONEY, EAT BETTER, IMPRESS EVERYONE

Cooking isn't just a skill; it's a form of independence. When you know your way around the kitchen, you're not at the mercy of overpriced restaurants or questionable takeout. Instead, you've got the freedom to whip up whatever your heart desires. Imagine customizing your meals exactly to your taste, swapping out ingredients to fit your preferences or dietary needs. Maybe you're into spicy dishes or love experimenting with flavors; cooking lets you do all this and more. Plus, when you cook, you're the boss of your plate. You decide how much salt goes in, what your veggies are, and whether you want to drizzle a little extra sauce.

Saving money is another huge perk. Dining out regularly can eat up your budget faster than you'd think. By learning to cook, you can stretch your dollars further. You can buy ingredients in bulk, use leftovers creatively, and plan meals to avoid unnecessary waste. It's about being smart with your resources, turning basic ingredients into delicious dishes that cost a fraction of what you'd pay elsewhere. This financial savvy helps you save and allows you to allocate funds towards other priorities, like those new shoes you've been eyeing or that concert you'd like to see.

There's also a **health** factor. Cooking at home means you control portion sizes and nutritional content. It's easier to eat balanced meals when you're the one deciding what's on the menu. You can incorporate more fruits, veggies, and whole grains, keeping your diet varied and nutritious. Plus, cooking can be a great stress reliever. It's a creative outlet, a chance to unplug and engage all your senses. The process of chopping, stirring, and tasting can be meditative, helping you unwind after a hectic day.

Let's not forget the **social** aspect. Sharing food is a universal way of connecting with others. Whether you're hosting a dinner party or just cooking for your roommates, preparing and enjoying meals together strengthens bonds. It's an opportunity to learn from each other, share recipes, and create memories. Cooking doesn't have to be a solo endeavor; it can be something you do with others, turning meal prep into a fun group activity. As you dive into cooking, remember it's not just about nourishment but also about fostering **independence, creativity, and connections.**

BASIC COOKING TECHNIQUES

Cooking might seem like a mysterious art at first, but it's a skill you can easily learn with practice, just like riding a bike.

- Let's start with **boiling**, the go-to method for pasta, rice, and eggs. It's simple: heat water until it's bubbling, add a dash of salt for flavor, then toss in your ingredients.
- **Steaming** is another beginner-friendly technique. It's like boiling but with much less water, so the steam cooks the food, not the water, keeping veggies crisp and nutrient-rich. Use a pot with a steaming rack or a microwave-safe dish with a lid —perfect for a quick side dish.
- **Sautéing** is where things get sizzling. A bit of oil in a hot pan gives you the perfect environment to cook meats and veggies quickly. The trick is to use a non-stick pan, make sure your pan is hot before adding the oil, and keep the food moving by stirring or tossing it frequently to ensure even cooking without burning.
- **Roasting** is ideal for savory foods like veggies, chicken, or fish. It uses higher temperatures (usually 400°F or more) to create a caramelized, crispy exterior. Toss ingredients with oil and seasonings, spread them on a baking sheet and a baking sheet, and let the oven work its magic. For easy cleanup, line the pan with foil or parchment paper.
- **Baking** is perfect for more delicate and precise dishes like cookies, cakes, or casseroles. It uses moderate temperatures (typically 325–375°F) to cook evenly and gently. Just follow the recipe closely, and your baked goods will come out beautifully.
- **Grilling** is where you get that smoky, charred flavor. Whether on an outdoor grill or an indoor grill pan, grilling adds a unique texture and taste to meats and vegetables. Make sure the grill is hot before placing your food, and use tongs to flip

and rotate for even cooking. Pro tip: marinate your food beforehand for extra flavor.

Practice your **knife skills**. The most important thing to remember is to **keep your fingers curled against the blade** when chopping to avoid accidents. Once you get the hang of slicing, dicing, and chopping, you'll prep your meals faster and more safely.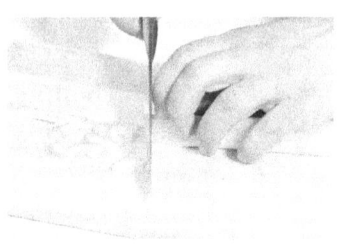
Always use a sharp knife; it's actually safer than a dull one, so investing in a basic knife sharpener to keep your knives sharp is a good idea. Some basic culinary knife cuts include:

- **Chop**: Rough, uneven bite-size pieces—great for when appearance doesn't matter.
- **Dice**: Uniform cubes, usually small, medium, or large depending on the recipe.
- **Mince**: Very small, fine pieces, typically used for garlic, herbs, or shallots.
- **Julienne**: Thin matchstick-like strips, ideal for vegetables like carrots or peppers.
- **Slice**: Thin, even cuts, often used for fruits, vegetables, and meats.

Meats like chicken, beef, and pork should be cooked thoroughly with no pink in the center. A **quick-read thermometer** is a handy tool to ensure they're done to the correct cooked temperature. Fish is quick-cooking; just a few minutes in a pan or oven until it flakes with a fork. And don't forget plant-based proteins like tofu, beans, and lentils. They're versatile and just need a good seasoning to shine.

Spices and herbs are essential for adding flavor to your dishes. Salt and pepper are just the beginning; mixing different seasonings can create endless flavor combinations. Crafting the perfect seasoning blend can be one of the trickiest parts of a recipe. If making your own blends seems overwhelming or costly due to the number of ingredients, pre-made sauces, spice mixes, and rubs are great alternatives. You can find **spice mixes and rubs** in the spices aisle of your supermarket and **bottled sauces and marinades** in the condiments or international foods aisle. Keep in mind that seasoning is all about balance—add a little at a time and taste as you go to avoid overdoing it.

Always read the recipe first to avoid surprises mid-cooking. Measure and prep all ingredients in advance so everything is ready to go. Stay focused at the stove, set a timer to prevent overcooking, and enjoy the process. Happy cooking!

COOKING HACKS: SHORTCUTS TO DELICIOUS AND STRESS-FREE MEALS

When time's tight, cooking hacks are your best friend. Start with **packaged meals**—they're not just for lazy nights. Add steamed broccoli or rotisserie chicken (which you can buy pre-cooked at most supermarkets) to boxed mac and cheese for a balanced meal. Crack an egg and toss in spinach with instant ramen, or mix frozen veggies and egg noodles into chicken broth for a quick soup. These simple upgrades can turn basic dishes into satisfying meals with minimal effort.

Prepping is another game-changer. Set aside an hour on the weekend to chop veggies, cook grains, or marinate your meats. This little bit of planning ahead can save you loads of time on busy weekdays. When you've got everything ready to go, throwing together a meal becomes as simple as mix-and-match. Just toss those prepped ingredients in a pan for a quick stir-fry or pop them in the oven for a sheet pan dinner. It's like having your own personal sous chef at the ready.

If you're not up for making sauces from scratch, no worries—**store-bought sauces** are your friends. Keep a few staples like spaghetti sauce or stir-fry sauce in your pantry, and you're halfway to a delicious meal. Just add your choice of fresh veggies or proteins, and dinner is served. For easy cleanup, **one-pot or sheet-pan meals** are perfect—just toss in ingredients, cook, and enjoy without a pile of dishes. Less mess, more time for you!

KITCHEN ESSENTIALS: MUST-HAVE TOOLS FOR EVERY HOME COOK

You don't need a top-of-the-line kitchen to whip up amazing meals. A few basic tools will set you on the path to culinary success.

- Let's start with a sharp **knife**. It's your ultimate tool for slicing, dicing, and chopping, and keeping it sharp is crucial for safety and efficiency so also have a basic **knife sharpener**. Pair it with a sturdy BPA-free plastic **cutting board**, ideal for meat and veg, to protect your counters and make prep work a breeze and safe to go in the dishwasher. **Potato peeler** and **cheese grater** are also incredibly helpful for speeding up these special tasks.
- A **non-stick fry pan** will become your go-to for eggs and veggies, while a **medium-sized pot** with a lid handles pasta and soups with ease. **Baking sheets** are versatile, and essential for everything from roasting veggies to baking cookies. And a **potholder** to protect your hands.
- **Mixing bowls** are another kitchen staple, ideal for everything from whipping up pancake batter to tossing salads. A 3-4

piece high-heat-resistant **silicone spatula set** is versatile for both prep and cooking and will not damage your non-stick pans.
- Precision matters in cooking, especially when baking, so **measuring cups and spoons** are essential. A **colander** is useful for straining pasta and rinsing veggies. And if you're new to cooking meats, an **instant-read thermometer** ensures everything is perfectly cooked.

When it comes to appliances, though not essential, a few handy gadgets can make meal prep a snap. These can be great gifts from family.

- The **microwave** isn't just for heating leftovers; it's also great for steaming veggies and cooking quick meals.
- A **rice cooker** can perfectly cook grains and double as a steamer for fish and veggies. Or an **Instant Pot**—It's a multi-tasking marvel that can also act as a slow cooker or pressure cooker, great for big-batch stews.
- An **air fryer** is another game-changer, using less oil to achieve that perfect crisp on chicken tenders or veggies, and cooks faster than a full-sized oven. Plus, it can reheat leftovers without making them soggy.
- A **blender** is a nice luxury, perfect for smoothies, sauces, creamed soups, and even grinding oats into flour. Whether you go for a personal blender or an immersion blender, choose one that suits your space and needs.

HEALTHY EATING MADE EASY

When it comes to healthy eating, think of your plate as a colorful canvas. A **balanced diet** isn't just about cutting calories or sticking to a rigid plan; it's about variety and ensuring your body gets what it needs to function at its best. Imagine dividing your plate into sections like a pie chart. Half of it should be loaded with veggies, bursting with color and nutrients. Whether it's a salad, sauteed veggies, or roasted beets and carrots, these provide essential vitamins and fiber that keep you feeling full and satisfied. The next quarter of your plate belongs to proteins, whether meat, tofu, or beans. Protein is crucial for muscle repair and growth, so aim for a portion about the size of your palm. The remaining quarter is for carbs, like whole grains, rice, or pasta, offering the energy you need to power through your day. Visualizing your meals this way helps ensure you get a balanced mix of everything your body craves.

Portion control is another important piece of the puzzle. Healthy eating is not just about what you eat but also how much. Learn to estimate portions: a serving of protein is about the size of your palm and carbs about the size of your fist. Remember, it takes 20 minutes to feel full, so sticking to portions helps prevent overeating while still enjoying your favorite foods. This way, you can indulge guilt-free and maintain healthy habits long-term.

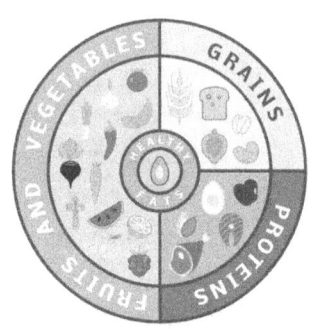

Remember to check the **nutritional info** on food labels. Note serving sizes and compare them to your portions. Choose options low in added sugars and high in protein and fiber to stay full longer. Knowing what's in your food helps you make choices that support your health goals.

QUICK AND EASY MEAL IDEAS

Mornings can be hectic, but quick **breakfast** options help.

- Start with toast—use bread, bagels, or English muffins. Add peanut butter for protein, or avocado for creaminess. Baked beans, a sausage patty, or a fried egg make for savory choices.

- Oatmeal is versatile—add raisins, dried dates, or nuts for crunch.
- For a lighter meal, top yogurt or cottage cheese with fruits like berries or bananas

Lunchtime can be simple.

- Leftovers are the easiest option—no extra prep is needed.
- If you want something different, try a soup and sandwich combo. Pile sandwiches with deli meats, cheese, salad greens or lettuce leaf, and your favorite condiments. For a warm twist, grill or toast it.
- Quesadillas, burritos, and wraps are quick and versatile - stuff them with cheese, rice, beans, or leftover meats and veggies. Add salsa or your favorite sauce to switch up the flavors.

Keeping healthy **snacks** on hand helps you avoid reaching for donuts or chips during mid-afternoon cravings.

- Try crackers or fresh veggies with hummus, or hard-boiled eggs for a protein boost.
- Nuts are another great option with healthy fats to keep you energized.
- For something sweeter, apple slices with a little peanut butter are a perfect combo.

Dinner can be stress-free, even on busy days.

- Stir-frying is a quick and flavorful way to make a delicious meal. Start by slicing your protein, like beef or tofu, and cook it thoroughly in a hot pan before adding the veggies. Once the meat is done, toss in your choice of vegetables—broccoli, carrots, zucchini, mushrooms, onions, or bell peppers all work great. Finish with a sauce you love, like teriyaki or pad

Thai, and serve over rice or noodles for a tasty, well-balanced dish.
- For something a bit different, try a DIY grain bowl. Start with a base of rice, couscous, or quinoa, and top it with roasted veggies such as Brussels sprouts, beets, butternut squash, and sweet potatoes. Add leftover grilled meat or tofu if you like, and finish with some salad greens and a splash of salad dressing.
- Fried rice is perfect for using up leftover rice and various remaining bits at the end of the week. Chop everything small, add scrambled egg, and season with stir-fry sauce.
- One-pot chili made with ground turkey and beans is hearty and comforting. Soups are also great for a simple dinner, especially when you add beans and hearty greens like kale to make them more filling.
- And if you want to keep cleanup minimal, go for sheet pan meals like fajitas with chicken, peppers, and onions. Just toss with fajita or taco seasoning, bake everything together, and enjoy.

MEAL PLANNING LIKE A PRO: STAY ORGANIZED, SAVE TIME, EAT BETTER

Imagine having your meals sorted for the entire week without the daily stress of deciding what's for dinner. Creating a meal plan is like setting up a playlist for your week—it saves you time, keeps your budget in check, and reduces food waste. Start by jotting down a list of dinners you'd like to make. Think versatile dishes that can do double duty, like a hearty pasta you can remix for lunch or a stir-fry that turns into a wrap the next day. Planning ahead makes you less likely to be tempted by costly takeout or impulse buys at the grocery store. It's about making your life easier, one meal at a time.

When you're just starting out, keep it simple. Choose recipes with a handful of ingredients that you can whip up without breaking a sweat.

Pasta dishes, stir-fries, and tacos are fantastic staples. They're easy to customize and forgiving if you don't get everything perfect the first time. The key is to focus on dishes that you enjoy eating and feel confident making. As you build your skills, you can start experimenting with more complex recipes. But for now, simplicity is your best friend.

Batch cooking and meal prepping are your secret weapons. Spend a little time on the weekend to cook a big pot of soup or make a family-sized lasagna. Portion them out into containers, and you've got meals ready to go for the week. Not only does this save you time, but it also ensures you have something delicious and homemade at your fingertips, even on the busiest days. Plus, it's a lifesaver when you come home tired and hungry with zero energy to cook.

Think of ingredients like bell peppers and chicken as building blocks. They're super versatile—you can roast peppers for a salad, toss them in fajitas, or stir-fry them with some tofu. Using the same ingredients across different meals helps reduce waste and keeps your meals from getting boring. It's about being creative and resourceful, using what you have to its full potential. This approach makes meal planning more efficient and adds variety to your diet without extra effort.

SMART GROCERY SHOPPING: STRATEGIES TO SAVE MONEY AND AVOID WASTE

Grocery shopping can feel like a daunting mission, especially when balancing budget and healthy choices. Start by embracing seasonal produce—it's fresher, tastier, and usually cheaper. Think juicy summer peaches or crisp fall apples.

For pantry staples like grains, coffee, cooking oil, and laundry detergent, when you're starting to get low, start watching out for sales and buy them when they're on sale. Choose store brands—they're usually the same quality as name brands but cost less.

Be flexible with your plans—if ham and bagels are on sale instead of turkey and bread, switch it up to save money.

As you stroll through the aisles, stick to the outer edges of the store. That's where you'll find fresh produce, dairy, and meats. These are the heart of healthy meals. The middle aisles are packed with processed foods and unhealthy snacks that can sneakily inflate your grocery bill without offering much nutritional value.

Planning is key. Before you even set foot in the store, have a game plan. Think about what meals you'll cook for the week. This is where meal planning, maximizing re-use of ingredients to ensure you consume everything you buy, comes into play and makes life so much easier. Write down everything you need. Stay focused and stick to your list when shopping; impulse buys can ruin your budget and lead to excess wasted food.

YOUR FIRST MEAL PLAN: A SAMPLE MENU AND SHOPPING LIST TO GET STARTED

	MON	TUES	WED	THURS	FRI	SAT	SUN
BREAKFAST	Toast with fried egg	Oatmeal with peanut butter	Avocado toast	Cottage cheese and fruit	Toast with peanut butter	Pancakes, Ham and cheese scramble	Spinach and mushroom scramble (+salsa)
LUNCH	Ham and cheese sandwich	Leftovers	Grain bowl using leftovers	Ham and avocado sandwich	Leftovers	Wrap/Tacos (+salsa)	Ramen with egg and spinach
SNACKS	Cottage cheese and fruit	Hard-boiled egg	Nuts	Crackers and cheese	Veggie and hummus	Fruit	Nuts
DINNER	Tofu stir fry with rice	Sheet pan roasted veg and chicken	Takeout or leftovers	Chili with ground beef; and salad	Mac and cheese with chicken and broccoli	Spaghetti, meatballs, and salad	Fried rice using all remaining leftovers

SHOPPING LIST

For This Week's Meals

Aisles
- [ ] Coffee
- [ ] Quick-cook instant oatmeal*
- [ ] Peanut butter*
    - for breakfast with toast/oatmeal, snack
- [ ] Nuts (walnuts or almonds)*
- [ ] 1 can 15oz stewed tomatoes*
    - for chili
- [ ] 1 can 29oz tomato sauce*
    - for chili
- [ ] 1 can 15oz black beans*
    - for chili
- [ ] 1 can 15oz red kidney beans
    - for chili
- [ ] 1 box mac and cheese
- [ ] 2 packs ramen
- [ ] 1 box spaghetti
- [ ] 1 jar spaghetti sauce*

Bakery
- [ ] Sandwich bread
    - for breakfast and sandwiches
- [ ] Tortilla
    - for lunch wrap, quesadilla, breakfast burrito

Produce:
- [ ] Fruit: in season and on sale
    - for breakfast and snacks
- [ ] Avocado
    - for toast, wrap, salad
- [ ] Salad greens or green leaf lettuce
    - for salad, sandwiches, tacos, wraps, grain bowl
- [ ] Spinach – can be eaten fresh or sauteed
    - for salad, scramble, ramen
- [ ] Tomatoes (2-4)
    - for salad, sandwiches, chili
- [ ] Broccoli (2 heads)
    - for stir-fry, chicken mac&cheese, roasted veg for grain bowl, fried rice
- [ ] Bell peppers (1-2)
    - for stir-fry, roasted veg, salad, chili, fried rice

- [ ] Carrots (1-2lbs)
    - for stir-fry, roasted veg, salad, snack with hummus, fried rice
- [ ] Cucumber (1)
    - for salad, snack with hummus, lunch wrap
- [ ] Red onions (1-2)
    - for stir-fry, sandwiches, chili, roasted veg, fried rice
- [ ] Zucchini (1-2)
    - for stir-fry, roasted veg, fried rice,
- [ ] Brussels sprouts or squash
    - for roasted veg and grain bowl
- [ ] Mushrooms
    - for stir-fry, scramble, grain bowl, fried rice

Refrigerated/Frozen
- [ ] Eggs
    - for breakfast, snack (hard-boiled), ramen, fried rice
- [ ] Milk
- [ ] Deli ham
    - for sandwiches, breakfast scramble
- [ ] Cheddar cheese 8oz block*
    - for breakfast scramble, sandwiches, chili, quesadilla
- [ ] Cottage cheese
    - for breakfast, snack
- [ ] Hummus
    - for snacks, lunch wrap
- [ ] Salsa
    - for breakfast, wraps, tacos, quesadilla
- [ ] Chicken (2lbs; 1lb per dish): boneless, skinless breast, thighs, or tenderloin
    - for sheet-pan with roasted veg, and mac&cheese
- [ ] Ground beef or plant-based crumbles (2lbs; 1lb per dish) for chili, meatballs
- [ ] Firm tofu
    for stir-fry

*normally available in store brands at lower price

Other Pantry and Fridge Staples

Aisles

- [ ] Pancake mix
- [ ] Pancake syrup
- [ ] Italian salad dressing
  - for salad; also use as a marinade for roasted veg
- [ ] Grill mates chicken seasoning (powder)
  - for sheet-pan chicken
- [ ] Teriyaki sauce
  - for stir-fry, fried rice
- [ ] Rice - white, brown, or grain blend
- [ ] Cooking oil*
- [ ] Package of cookies or box of brownies to bake - on sale
  - special treat

These items last a long time, and you wouldn't normally have this many items to buy in one week

Non-Food, Other Household Essentials

Aisles

- [ ] Laundry detergent
- [ ] Dishwashing soap
- [ ] Shampoo

This week's meal plan costs around $110. Plan on an extra $10-$20 for items like condiments, seasonings, and other pantry staples that last several weeks; spread these purchases out over many weeks, so you're not spending too much on any given week. Occasionally, budget an additional $10-$20 for household essentials like cleaning supplies and toiletries. Choosing store brands helps cut costs, and as you get better at cooking, you can swap ingredients or recipes to use sale items and save even more.

If you have leftover ingredients like spaghetti sauce, pasta, tortillas, or cheese, incorporate them into next week's meal plan to avoid waste!

ACTION PLAN

Let's put all this into action with a meal plan for the week.

1. **Find Your Go-To Recipes:** Start by picking 3-5 dishes you love—think a big pot of chili or a hearty pasta dish. Keep it simple, so you can build your skills and confidence in the kitchen. Use easy cooking hacks to make it even better!

2. **Plan Out Your Meals:** Make a meal plan for the week, balancing proteins, carbs, and veggies, and aim to reuse ingredients to save money and time.

   - Pick one or two cooking techniques to master this week, like boiling for soup or sautéing for a quick stir-fry. These are the building blocks for so many recipes!
   - Plan a social hangout, like a potluck or group meal where everyone brings ingredients. It's a fun way to connect, support each other, and share costs.

3. **Make a Smart Shopping List:** Use your hand to eyeball portions so you know how much to buy, and jot down everything you need.

   - Check your pantry first so you're not buying what you already have. Swap pricey meats for affordable options like beans or lentils if needed.
   - Stick to your list—impulse buys can wreck your budget! Remember, money saved = more cash for things you really want.

4. **Prep Like a Pro:** Sharpen your knife, wash and chop veggies, and get everything ready for the week or at least the next few days.

5. **Read, Watch, and Learn:** Read the recipe before you start cooking and have all your ingredients laid out. If you're trying something new, watch a quick YouTube video before starting. To find the best instructional videos on YouTube, type *"How to _____ for Beginners - YouTube."* Fill in the blank with whatever you want to learn, like "boil water and cook pasta," "steam vegetables," "sauté veggies or meat," "roast chicken breast in a pan," or "cook perfect scrambled eggs."

6. **Get Cooking & Enjoy!** Time to put your plan into action. Enjoy cooking, share it with friends, and most importantly, have fun in the kitchen! Happy eating!

3

HEALTH, HYGIENE, AND WELLNESS FUNDAMENTALS

Now, let's take care of *you*! This chapter dives into everything from personal hygiene and healthy eating to physical fitness and mental wellness. These aren't just boring routines; they're your daily power moves to feel your best, inside and out. We'll cover the basics of staying fresh, fueling your body with the right foods, staying active, and keeping your mind sharp and stress-free. Whether you're looking to boost your confidence, energy, or mood, this chapter will give you the tools to build habits that help you thrive!

PERSONAL HYGIENE ESSENTIALS: STAY FRESH, STAY CONFIDENT

As you move from adolescence to adulthood, your body goes through many changes, mainly because of hormones. These changes can impact your skin, teeth, and overall hygiene, making it more important to take care of yourself. Simple routines like washing your face and brushing your teeth play a bigger role in keeping you healthy and feeling your best. Establishing solid hygiene habits now sets the foundation for a healthy lifestyle. Let's start with the basics: daily routines. Think of your hygiene routine as the ultimate self-care ritual.

- **Teeth**. Brush your teeth twice a day with fluoride toothpaste—once when you wake up and again before bed. Use a soft toothbrush to protect your gums from receding. It might sound like common sense, but brushing is your #1 weapon against cavities and bad breath. And don't skip flossing. It reaches those tight spots your toothbrush can't handle. Plus, hit up the dentist for check-ups and cleanings every six months. Catching problems early can save you from painful stuff later (like root canals—yikes!). If you're always battling dental issues, think about upgrading to an electric toothbrush and making flossing a daily habit.
- **Handwashing** might seem like a no-brainer, but it's one of the easiest ways to stay healthy. Always wash your hands before eating or preparing food, after using the bathroom, after coughing, sneezing, or blowing your nose, after touching garbage, before and after caring for someone who's sick, after handling animals or cleaning up after them, before and after treating a wound or cut, and after being in public spaces like using public transportation, touching handrails, or door handles. Washing your hands for at least 20 seconds with soap and water is the best way to keep germs and diseases from spreading!
- When it comes to **bathing**, find a routine that fits your lifestyle. Regular showers wash away dirt, sweat, and bacteria, keeping you fresh and preventing body odor. But you don't always need to shampoo and condition daily. If your hair is oily, you might wash it more often, while dry or curly hair can benefit from less frequent washing. Your skin needs attention too, so create a skincare routine that includes cleansing, moisturizing, and sunblock. The products you choose should match your skin and hair type—whether oily, dry, or sensitive. And if you're dealing with tough skin issues like acne, don't hesitate to get professional advice or try a targeted skincare routine.

- Don't skip **nail care**—your nails can say a lot about your hygiene habits. Keep them trimmed and clean to stop dirt and bacteria from collecting underneath. If you love nail polish, remember to give your nails a break occasionally so they can stay healthy, recover from any damage, and avoid issues like brittle nails, yellowing, or fungal infections. And don't forget to moisturize your hands regularly; they work hard every day and deserve some TLC!

Good hygiene isn't just about looking good, though that's a nice bonus. It's about feeling good and knowing you're taking the best possible care of your body, inside and out.

FUEL YOUR BODY RIGHT: SIMPLE AND SMART HEALTHY EATING HABITS

Let's talk about food—the stuff that powers you up, keeps your brain sharp, and makes you feel awesome. Eating isn't just about filling your stomach; it's about giving your body what it needs to crush the day. Think of a **balanced diet** like the ultimate playlist, with the perfect mix of proteins, carbs, and fats to keep everything running smoothly. Proteins are the building blocks—whether you're eating chicken, lentils, or tofu, they're helping your body grow and repair itself. Carbs? They're your main energy source, fueling everything from homework to sports. Go for whole grains like brown rice or quinoa to keep your energy steady. And healthy fats? They're like the DJs of your diet—avocados, nuts, and olive oil add flavor and help your body absorb those key vitamins.

But it's not just about what you eat—it's also about how you eat. **Mindful eating** is key. It means paying attention to your food and really savoring each bite. It's about knowing when you're hungry and recognizing when you're full. By eating mindfully, you can actually enjoy your meals more and avoid overeating. Try ditching the distractions, like your phone or TV, so you can focus on your food and listen to what your body is telling you. Eating slowly and savoring each bite not only makes meals more satisfying, but also helps you stay in tune with your hunger cues and prevents mindless snacking that can add many pounds over time. Mindful eating is all about being present with your food!

Hydration is another piece of the puzzle. Water is your body's unsung hero, playing a critical role in everything from digestion to regulating body temperature. Aim to drink plenty of water throughout the day and pay attention to your thirst signals. Carrying a reusable water bottle can serve as a reminder to stay hydrated. And while sugary drinks might be tempting, they can sneak in extra calories without filling you up. Opt for water or unsweetened beverages whenever you can. If you enjoy a bit of flavor, infuse your water with slices of lemon, or a splash of your favorite juice or kombucha for a refreshing twist.

Eating healthy doesn't mean giving up your favorite treats—it's all about **balance and moderation**. If you're craving something sweet or indulgent, go for it! Just keep portions in check, and you'll find that even three bites can be enough to satisfy that craving. Treats can fit into a balanced diet without throwing off your health goals. The key is making healthier choices most of the time and not stressing over the occasional indulgence. Food is meant to be enjoyed, not something to stress about. Remember the guideline from Chapter 2, which gives you a visual way to balance your plate by allocating fruits, veggies, proteins, and grains. Keeping these tips in mind will help you create nutritious and satisfying meals every day!

Healthy eating is about making choices that nourish your body and mind. It's about finding a rhythm that fits your lifestyle and makes you feel your best. So, as you explore the world of nutrition, remember to keep it simple. Focus on whole, fresh foods, listen to your body, don't eat too much, and enjoy discovering what works best for you.

MOVE IT TO IMPROVE IT: PHYSICAL ACTIVITY FOR ENERGY AND STRENGTH

Imagine waking up every day feeling energized and ready to crush whatever's on your to-do list. That's just one of the many perks of regular **exercise**. It's not just about getting in shape—it's like a magic ticket to a healthier, happier life. When you move your body, you're giving your heart a workout, boosting your **cardiovascular health**, and **building strength**. Plus, the benefits go way beyond the physical. Exercise is a serious **mood booster**, flooding your body with endorphins that leave you feeling happier and less stressed. It can also help you **sleep better** and **sharpen your memory**, giving you an edge at school or work. And let's be real—being fit doesn't just feel good, it looks good too, and that boost in confidence is a nice bonus!

Now, let's explore the types of exercise and how each one can fit into your routine.

- **Cardio** is your go-to for getting your heart racing. Whether running, swimming, cycling, or dancing, these activities do wonders for your cardiovascular health while torching calories. Think of cardio as an adrenaline boost for your heart, keeping it strong and healthy.
- Then there's **strength training**, where you build muscle and boost bone density. You can lift weights, use resistance bands, or do bodyweight exercises like push-ups and squats. It's a must-have in your routine because it helps you tone up and rev up your metabolism.
- And don't forget **flexibility** exercises like yoga, Pilates, and stretching. These moves increase your range of motion, reduce stiffness, and prevent injuries. Plus, they're key for maintaining balance and coordination, making everyday activities smoother and more fun!

Creating a **fitness plan** that fits your lifestyle is all about setting goals that work for you and finding activities you actually enjoy. You don't need to train for a marathon, but try to get at least 30 minutes of moderate activity each day. As you get stronger and fitter, you can step up the intensity, length, or frequency of your workouts. This keeps things interesting and challenging without burning you out. The key is balance—mix in cardio, strength, and flexibility exercises throughout the week to hit all the important areas. Fitness apps like Nike Training Club or 7 Minute Workout are awesome for guiding your workouts and tracking progress. Plus, they offer tons of routines and keep you motivated with challenges and support from their community!

Staying motivated can be tough, but there are plenty of tricks to keep you going. Find an exercise buddy or join a fitness group. Working out with others can be a great way to stay accountable and make exercise more fun. Music is another powerful motivator. Create a playlist of your favorite tunes or listen to podcasts and audiobooks while you work out. It's a great way to make the time fly by. Lastly, integrate fitness into your daily life. Park farther from your destination to sneak in extra steps or take the stairs instead of the elevator. Even small actions like carrying a backpack while walking the dog can double as strength training. If you have the option, ride your bike instead of driving. These little changes add up, making physical activity a seamless part of your routine.

MIND OVER MATTER: MANAGING STRESS, ANXIETY, AND EMOTIONAL WELLNESS

Understanding your **mental health** is just as important as taking care of your physical health. Stress and anxiety, two familiar culprits, can sometimes feel like a heavy weight on your shoulders. They often get lumped together, but they have differences. Stress is usually that tight feeling in your chest before a big exam or when you're juggling too many responsibilities at once. It's that pressure that comes and goes with life's demands. Anxiety, on the other hand, is like stress's intense cousin. It's that nagging feeling of worry or fear that hangs around, even when there's no immediate threat. Both can mess with your head and body, causing everything from headaches and tension to sleepless nights and irritability.

Being **emotionally aware** is a superpower that helps you navigate these feelings. It starts with recognizing and naming your emotions. Are you feeling overwhelmed, anxious, or just plain tired? Once you identify it, accepting your emotions without judgment is key. It's okay to feel what you're feeling. The next step is learning to express these emotions in a healthy way—whether that means talking it out with a friend, writing it down in a journal, or even channeling it into something creative. Emotionally aware people don't let their feelings control them. Instead, they use their emotions as a guide to understand themselves better.

Identifying what triggers your stress or anxiety is like finding pieces to a puzzle. Maybe it's that looming deadline, a packed schedule, or even social situations. Whatever it is, **knowing your triggers** can help you develop strategies to manage or avoid them. This doesn't mean running away from challenges but finding ways to cope. Maybe it's scheduling some downtime after a hectic week or practicing saying no to commitments that overload you. Being proactive about your mental health can make all the difference.

Coping strategies are your toolkit for handling tough emotions, whether it's stress, anxiety, or feeling overwhelmed.

- **Regular exercise** is a game-changer—it releases endorphins that boost your mood and energy.
- **Mindfulness** practices like meditation, journaling, or deep breathing can help calm your mind and center your thoughts.
- Even simple things like spending time in **nature** or diving into a **hobby** can work wonders.

- Don't underestimate the power of a **balanced diet** and **good sleep**—they seriously impact your mood and focus.
- **Cognitive reframing** is another great tool—it helps you shift your perspective by turning negative thoughts into more positive or constructive ones. Instead of seeing a challenge as a failure, you reframe it as a learning opportunity.
- **Managing your time effectively** can prevent stress from piling up.
- Having a **solid support system** of friends and family can provide comfort, and engaging in spiritual practices or communities can add a sense of connection.
- It's important to **avoid unhealthy coping mechanisms** like substance abuse or excessive eating, which can lead to more stress in the long run.

Find what works best for you, build a routine that supports your well-being, and **be kind to yourself** on tough days. Remember, **you're not alone**—almost everyone experiences stress and anxiety at some point. **Reaching out for support** is a sign of strength, not weakness. Whether it's a friend, family member, or a mental health professional, there's always someone ready to listen and help.

Taking care of your mental health is super important because it impacts everything—how you think, feel, and act. When your mind is in a good place, you're better at handling stress, building strong friendships, and making smart decisions. It's like giving yourself the tools to crush challenges and live your best life. Ignoring your mental health, though, can lead to issues like anxiety, depression, burnout, and even physical problems. Just like hitting the gym for your body, your mind needs care too, and when you prioritize it, you're setting yourself up to thrive in every part of your life!

NAVIGATING DOCTORS AND MEDICAL CARE: WHAT YOU NEED TO KNOW

As you dive into adulthood, taking care of your health becomes your responsibility. It might sound intimidating, but it's really about knowing a few basics to keep yourself in check.

Step one: get yourself a **primary care doctor**. This is your go-to doctor —the person you'll go to for regular check-ups and anything weird that pops up. Even if you feel fine, don't skip your annual check-up—these visits are a chance to make sure everything's working the way it should and to get ahead of any health issues before they become big problems. **Vaccines** aren't just for kids—make sure you're up-to-date on shots like the flu or HPV vaccine.

If something specific comes up, you might need to see a **specialist**. Skin problem? That's a **dermatologist**. Questions about birth control, reproductive health, or menstrual issues? Head to a **gynecologist**. And don't forget mental health—seeing a **therapist** or **psychiatrist** for stress or anxiety is just as important as checking in with a physical health doctor.

If you have **health insurance**, take a minute to figure out what's covered—this includes how to book appointments and what your co-pays are. If you don't have insurance, look into local clinics that offer affordable care. You may also qualify for **Affordable Care Act plans, Medicaid, or other government health programs**, which provide low-cost or free coverage based on income. Understanding how it all works will save you a lot of hassle later.

Urgent care vs. emergency room—it's important to know the difference. **Urgent care** is for things like sprains, minor infections, or when you need quick help but it's not life-threatening. The **ER** is for serious emergencies, like chest pain, difficulty breathing, or severe injuries. Knowing where to go in a pinch will save you time and get you the right care quickly.

Keep your **health records** handy—stuff like medications, allergies, past conditions, and procedures. It'll make doctor visits easier, and you'll get better care when everything's in one place.

Listen to Your Body. If something feels off, don't ignore it. Whether it's a weird pain or changes in mood, trust your gut and see a doctor. It's always better to catch things early.

If you're prescribed **medications**, follow the instructions. Even if you feel better, don't stop taking them early unless your doctor says so. Stick to the plan and stay informed about side effects.

Taking care of your health is about being proactive. Find a doctor, stay on top of check-ups, and don't hesitate to reach out if something doesn't feel right. Your health is in your hands, and these basics will help you navigate adulthood with confidence!

ACTION PLAN

Let's put all of this into action:

1. **Review Your Health and Hygiene Routine**

- Take a look at your current personal hygiene habits. Are there areas that need updating? Whether it's brushing, flossing, or skin care, keeping these basics in check is important.

2. **Plan Your Meals for the Week**

- Review Chapter 2 and create a balanced meal plan for the week. Aim to include a mix of fruits, veggies, proteins, and whole grains that support your energy and well-being.

3. Get Moving

- Are you hitting at least 30 minutes of physical activity each day or 3.5 hours per week? If not, it's time to shake things up! You don't need a gym membership to get moving. A brisk walk on your lunch break, dancing, or biking are all easy options. Even small changes, like taking the stairs or parking further away, can add up. Start simple and see how much movement you can sneak into your routine.

4. Check-In on Your Mental Health

- How's your current mental state? What coping strategies are you using, and are they actually working for you? Take a moment to assess what's helping and what's not. If something isn't effective, try exploring new techniques like mindfulness, exercise, journaling, or talking to a trusted friend. The key is to find at least three solid strategies that genuinely help you feel better and that you can rely on when needed.

5. Get Up to Date on Healthcare

- When was your last dentist appointment? If it's been more than a year, schedule a cleaning and check-up.
- Have you seen your primary care physician recently? Make sure to get a regular check-up and update your vaccines.
- Start a simple health record in your note-taking app—vaccines, conditions, medications, and allergies—so you have easy access when you need it.

6. Nurture Your Social Connections

- Do you have a supportive social network? Take a moment to think about the relationships in your life.

- Reach out to someone important each week, whether it's a quick text or a coffee catch-up. These connections are essential for your mental health, providing support, joy, and balance.
- If you feel like your social circle needs some growth, consider joining a club, volunteering, or getting involved in activities you enjoy to meet like-minded people.

Putting these steps into practice will help you maintain your physical, mental, and social well-being, setting you up for a balanced and fulfilling life!

4

TIME MANAGEMENT AND MAXIMIZING PRODUCTIVITY

MASTERING TIME MANAGEMENT

It's a late Sunday night, and you're staring at a mountain of tasks that all seem to demand your attention at once. Between school projects, part-time jobs, and trying to maintain some semblance of a social life, it feels like you're juggling more balls than you have hands for. Sound familiar? You're not alone.

Managing time effectively can feel overwhelming, but think of it like leveling up in a video game—once you master the right strategies and tools, you'll navigate your days with more ease and control. Just like in a game, where better skills and resources unlock new abilities, strong time management helps reduce stress, boost productivity, and even free up more time for the things you actually enjoy.

One powerful way to tackle time management is by learning to **prioritize tasks effectively**, a skill that can transform chaos into order. Enter the **Eisenhower Matrix**, a productivity tool that categorizes tasks based on urgency and importance. Named after Dwight D. Eisenhower, this matrix helps you decide what to focus on first. Imagine a grid with four boxes: the first quadrant is for tasks that are both urgent and important, like studying for tomorrow's exam. These need immediate attention. The second quadrant covers important but not urgent tasks, such as a long-term research project. These tasks require planning and are crucial for achieving your goals but aren't pressing at the moment. The third quadrant is for urgent but unimportant tasks—like helping your roommate pick an outfit for tonight's date. These can often be delegated. Lastly, the fourth quadrant is for tasks that are neither urgent nor important, like endless scrolling on social media. These are time-wasters that should be minimized or avoided. Using this matrix, you can systematically prioritize your tasks, reducing stress and making sure you focus on what truly matters. This sense of control over your time is empowering and liberating.

	Urgent	Not Urgent
Important	DO FIRST ☐ Complete assignment due tomorrow	SCHEDULE ☐ Grocery shopping and meal prep
Not Important	DELEGATE OR SKIP ☐ Lengthy phone calls	AVOID ☐ Posting on social media

Once you've prioritized your tasks, consider using **timeboxing** to structure your schedule. With timeboxing, you assign fixed time slots to different activities, helping you maintain focus and avoid getting stuck on one task for too long. For example, you might block out two hours on Tuesday for writing your research paper, one hour on Thursday for test prep, and 30 minutes each evening for exercise or relaxation. By visually mapping out your tasks, you create a structured routine that balances productivity with downtime. The key to timeboxing is that when the time is up, you move on—whether the task is finished or not. This keeps you on track and prevents overworking any single task.

Now, let's talk about **procrastination**, that sneaky villain that often derails even the best-laid plans. One way to fight it is by using the **Pomodoro Technique**, which is all about working in short, structured bursts. Unlike timeboxing, where you allocate fixed time slots for tasks, Pomodoro is a cycle-based method designed to boost focus. Here's how it works: set a timer for 25 minutes, work with full focus, then take a five-minute break. After four work sessions (Pomodoros), take a longer 15-30 minute break. This method helps break overwhelming tasks into **manageable chunks**, making it easier to start and stay engaged without burning out.

If you're struggling with getting started, the **Two-Minute Rule** is another great hack—if a task takes less than two minutes, do it immediately. You'd be surprised how much you can load in the dishwasher in just two minutes! Whether you're using timeboxing for structure or Pomodoro for focus, these techniques can help you get more done with less stress and more motivation.

Batching tasks is another effective strategy for maximizing productivity. It's all about grouping similar tasks together to save time and mental energy. For example, instead of checking your emails sporadically throughout the day, set aside specific times to go through your inbox, reply to messages, and clear out the junk. The same goes for phone calls or any repetitive tasks. By handling similar tasks all at once, you reduce the disruption to your workflow, allowing for more sustained periods of focus on other projects. This approach not only saves time but also helps you feel more in control of your schedule. Other tasks that can be batched include meal preparation, laundry, and studying for multiple subjects.

Sara, a college student, has a term paper due in six weeks. Using the Eisenhower Matrix, she identifies it as important but not urgent (Quadrant 2) and applies timeboxing, scheduling two afternoons per week for focused work. Each session has a clear start and end time, ensuring she makes progress without letting the paper take over her entire schedule. To stay efficient, she batches tasks, dedicating specific time blocks for research, outlining, and writing, minimizing distractions, and avoiding the time lost switching between different types of work. She identifies social events and party planning as potential distractions, categorizing them in Quadrant 3 (urgent but not important). This helps her manage her time wisely. During study sessions, Sara uses the Pomodoro Technique, working in 25-minute intervals with short breaks to stay focused. By combining timeboxing for structure, batching for efficiency, and Pomodoro for concentration, she makes steady progress on her paper—while still making time for fun.

Weekly reviews are like your personal reset button. At the end of each week, take some time to reflect on what you've accomplished and what could use more attention. Review your tasks, assess what went well, and identify any areas where you might have gotten off track. This is your chance to reorganize your priorities for the upcoming week. Maybe you underestimated how long a particular project would take, or perhaps you found yourself distracted by unexpected obligations. Use these insights to adjust your plans, ensuring that your upcoming week is more streamlined and focused. This regular practice of reflection and adjustment helps you stay aligned with your goals, making each week a little more efficient than the last.

MASTERING ORGANIZATION: HACKS, APPS, AND TOOLS FOR A PRODUCTIVE LIFE

Creating an **organized environment** is like setting the stage for a productive day. Think about your workspace. Is it cluttered with papers, random knick-knacks, and a few half-empty coffee cups? A messy space can lead to a messy mind, making it harder to concentrate and get stuff done. Start by decluttering. Tidy up your desk, put away items you don't need, and keep only the daily use essentials within arm's reach. A clean, organized space not only reduces distractions but can also boost your mood and motivation. Imagine walking into a room where everything has its place; it instantly sets a positive tone for the day. It's like giving your brain a fresh start each time you sit down to work.

In today's digital age, organizing your digital space is just as crucial. With endless information coming at you from all angles, using **digital tools** can be a lifesaver. Everyone's got a phone, and it's probably glued to your hand most of the day. Why not make it work for you by using apps that help you stay organized?

When it comes to **managing tasks**, apps like Todoist, Notion, and Trello are like having personal assistants in your pocket. Each one shines in its own way. **Todoist** is perfect for keeping track of daily tasks and deadlines—you can organize tasks into projects, set priorities, and schedule reminders so nothing slips through the cracks. **Notion** takes organization to the next level with its all-in-one workspace, combining notes, to-do lists, and project trackers in a highly customizable layout that adapts to your workflow. Meanwhile, **Trello** is a dream for visual thinkers, using a board-and-card system to display tasks at a glance. You can drag cards from "To Do" to "In Progress" to "Done," making it easy (and super satisfying) to see your progress in real time.

Now, let's move on to **note-taking**. Whether you're in class, at work, or jotting down a random idea, the right app helps you easily capture and find these notes later. **Google Keep** is fantastic for quick, straightforward notes and checklists—it's simple, fast, and syncs across devices, so your ideas are always at your fingertips. If you need something more powerful, **Evernote** has you covered. It lets you organize notes into notebooks, attach files or images, and even save web pages for later. Both apps make sure your thoughts and ideas are safe, accessible, searchable, and ready to support you, whether you're collaborating on a group project or tackling solo tasks.

When it comes to **calendars, Google Calendar** is the ultimate go-to for organizing your life. It's more than just a place to track classes and appointments—it's a powerhouse for timeboxing, helping you allocate time for work, study, socializing, or self-care. You can use color coding to visually separate different parts of your life, making your schedule easy to read at a glance. Plus, it syncs seamlessly with apps like Todoist to keep your tasks and events perfectly aligned. Need to coordinate plans? Sharing calendars with friends, roommates, or teammates makes planning group events a breeze.

Sara, a busy college student juggling classes, her part-time job, and personal commitments, starts her day by checking **Google Calendar**. Her schedule is color-coded: blue for classes, green for work shifts, and yellow for personal time, making it easy to see what's on deck. Using timeboxing, she blocks out specific times for studying, working out, and social events, ensuring balance in her hectic life. To stay on track, she syncs **Todoist** with her calendar, so her to-dos—like "Finish essay draft" or "Prep for biology quiz"—are neatly integrated into her day. The reminders help her stick to her plan, even during the busiest weeks. Throughout the day, Sara uses **Evernote** to capture important details and stay organized. In class, she takes notes directly into her course-specific notebooks, which also house articles, scanned PDFs, and quick ideas for assignments. Later, during her study session (scheduled on her calendar), she reviews her notes and updates her Todoist tasks, breaking big assignments into smaller, manageable steps. By combining **Google Calendar** for scheduling, **Todoist** for task management, and **Evernote** for note-taking, Sara keeps everything in sync, improving her productivity and reducing stress.

Finding the right combination of apps to organize your life is a bit of trial and error, but that's part of the fun. Everyone's workflow is different, so it's worth experimenting with these tools or others to see what clicks for you. And remember, new apps are always hitting the market, offering fresh features to make life even easier. The key is to use these digital tools to work smarter, not harder—streamlining your tasks, improving efficiency, and cutting down on stress. Your phone isn't just for social media and memes; it can be your ultimate sidekick in staying on top of everything life throws your way!

> Take a moment to review your calendar and to-do lists and reflect on this week's accomplishments and any challenges you faced. What tasks took longer than expected? What surprised you? Use this reflection to plan for the week ahead—rearrange your priorities, block out time for tasks you underestimated, and identify three goals to focus on. Adjust your digital tools to reflect these changes and remove any unnecessary clutter from your workspace.

GOAL SETTING AND ACHIEVEMENT

Setting goals might seem like just another task on your already packed to-do list, but it's actually your secret weapon for staying motivated and focused. Goals give you a clear sense of direction, turning the random chaos of daily tasks into a path with purpose. When you have a goal, you have a target to aim for, and every step you take brings you closer to hitting that bullseye. However, not all goals are created equal. This is where the **SMART framework** comes in handy. SMART stands for Specific, Measurable, Achievable, Relevant, and Time-bound. For instance, if you're working on a term paper, don't just say, "I want to write a paper." Make it SMART: "I will research and write a 10-page paper on climate change impacts by April 10th, focusing on economic factors." Now you have a clear, trackable target.

Creating a goal plan is about **breaking down that big goal into bite-sized pieces**. It's like turning a mountain into a series of manageable hills. Start by listing out all the steps needed to achieve your goal, then organize them in a logical order. Keep it simple. If your big goal is to complete that term paper, smaller goals might include: "Research sources for two hours on Monday" and "Draft the introduction by next Friday." By focusing on these smaller, more achievable tasks, you can avoid feeling overwhelmed and make steady progress. Each small victory builds momentum, keeping you engaged and motivated.

Tracking your progress is like having a personal coach cheering you on and helping you stay on course. Use task management apps like Notion and Todoist or a simple spreadsheet to monitor your achievements and celebrate those small wins. Seeing your progress visually can be incredibly satisfying and motivating. It also gives you a chance to adjust your plan if something isn't working. Maybe you realize that researching takes longer than expected, and you need to allocate more time. Or perhaps you find a new resource that requires shifting priorities. Regularly reviewing and adjusting your goals ensures they remain relevant and realistic, adapting to any changes in your situation.

Consider Sara's approach to her term paper. She sets a SMART goal of completing a 15-page analysis on renewable energy policies by mid-May. Her plan involves creating a detailed timeline: by week two, she aims to complete her research; by week four, her first draft; and by week six, final edits and proofreading. Sara uses Todoist to track and log her daily progress, marking each completed task with a satisfying check. This visual cue helps her see how far she's come, keeping her spirits high and her focus sharp. When she notices she's falling behind, she adapts by dedicating more time on weekends. Through careful planning and regular adjustments, Sara not only stays on track but also reduces stress, finds joy in her work, and gains the confidence to tackle future challenges easily.

MULTITASKING: THE GOOD AND THE BAD

Multitasking might seem like a superhero skill—saving the day by getting more done in less time. Still, while it can be incredibly efficient in certain scenarios, it can also lead to more mistakes and less productivity overall. Think about trying to juggle too many things at once. It can feel like you're doing a lot, but in reality, you might be dropping the ball on something important. When you attempt to tackle multiple tasks simultaneously, it can divide your attention, making it harder to do any one thing well. Studies even show that our brains aren't really built for multitasking. We actually switch rapidly between tasks, which can be mentally exhausting and lead to errors.

However, when used strategically, multitasking can be beneficial. It's all about knowing when and how to use it. Combining complementary tasks is one way to make the most of multitasking without overwhelming yourself. For example, meal prepping while listening to a podcast related to a class project is a win-win. You're feeding your body and your brain at the same time. Or consider exercising with friends. You're not just burning calories but also catching up, which is a great way to socialize without sacrificing your fitness goals. Another idea is doing homework while waiting for your laundry to finish. You're making the most of your downtime, turning waiting into productive study time. These examples show that by **pairing activities that don't require the same type of focus**, you can get more done without feeling stretched too thin.

Batching tasks is another technique that can help. By grouping similar tasks, like answering emails or paying bills, you can stay in the zone and knock them out faster. The key is to avoid tasks that compete for the same mental resources. This way, you're not constantly switching gears, which can be mentally taxing. But remember, the quality of your work matters more than the quantity. Multitasking shouldn't come at the expense of doing things well. It's important to recognize when to focus on a single task, especially if it requires deep concentration or creativity.

Finally, remember that **collaboration** and **teamwork** can be just as powerful for managing workloads effectively. By delegating tasks based on individual strengths—like in a group project where one person handles research, another focuses on visuals, and someone else shines in presenting—you not only share the load but also elevate the final product. Strategic multitasking and collaboration are two strategies that help you work smarter, not harder, ensuring both productivity and quality in everything you do.

ACTION PLAN

1. **Set Clear Goals**:

   - **Define Your Goal**: Decide what you want to accomplish in the next three months—whether it's launching a blog, training for a half marathon, excelling in a course, or landing a new job.
   - **Break It Down into SMART Goals**:
   - Set daily, weekly, and monthly targets to keep yourself on track.
   - Example: Write 500 words daily, finish one chapter weekly, and complete a solid draft by the end of the month.
   - **Prioritize Wisely**: Use the **Eisenhower Matrix** to focus on what's most important, avoid distractions, and prevent overloading yourself. This ensures you're spending time on what truly moves you forward.

2. **Set Up and Use a Digital Toolkit**:

   - Choose one app for each task: **calendar**, **notes**, and **task management**.
   - Set them up by inputting goals, scheduling reminders, and organizing tasks.
   - Once set up, your digital toolkit acts like a personal assistant, helping you stay focused and on track without the mental clutter.

3. **Plan and Reflect Weekly**: Tackle daily tasks with intention.

- With your goals set and apps ready, it's time to dive into the week's objectives.
- Review your progress weekly:
    - Did you plan your goals and to-dos in manageable chunks?
    - Did you allocate enough time for tasks, or did distractions throw you off?
    - What worked, and what needs adjustment?
- Learn what worked and tweak what didn't for next week.

4. **Create a Cycle of Improvement**:

- Creating a cycle of improvement is like leveling up in a game —each round brings you closer to mastery. Plan your tasks into bite-sized pieces, crush them with focus, and then take a moment to reflect: What worked? What didn't? Notice patterns, like when you're in the zone or which tasks always take forever, and adjust to make life easier. Before you know it, what once felt impossible starts to feel totally doable. These habits aren't just for one project—they're lifelong tools to help you tackle goals and succeed in every area of your life.

5

CAREER PLANNING AND JOB SKILLS

FROM SEARCH TO SUCCESS: NAIL YOUR JOB HUNT

Imagine scrolling through your favorite social media feed and suddenly seeing a post about someone landing their dream job. You might feel a mix of excitement and envy, thinking, "How did they do it?" Well, you're about to find out. Job hunting is not just about sending out a flurry of applications and crossing your fingers. It's a journey of discovery, patience, and resilience, where each step teaches you something new about yourself and the job market. The process involves more than just clicking "apply." It's about researching companies, tailoring your applications, preparing for interviews, and sometimes facing rejection. And that's okay. Each "no" brings you closer to the "yes" that's meant for you.

When you start job hunting, it's crucial to enter with the right mindset. It's easy to get discouraged, especially when things don't go as planned. But remember, every successful career begins with someone taking that first uncertain step. Begin by researching companies and identifying roles that align with your interests and skills. Dive deep into understanding what these organizations stand for and what they offer. This not only helps you tailor your applications but also prepares you for interviews. Setting clear daily or weekly goals is essential. Aim to apply to a certain number of jobs each day or focus on improving your resume. This structured approach keeps you moving forward even when setbacks occur.

Preparation is vital to keeping your spirits high during the job hunt. Think of it as building a foundation for your future. Start by crafting a resume that highlights your strengths and skills. Even if you don't have formal work experience, consider including internships, volunteer work, or extracurricular activities that demonstrate your capabilities. Proofreading is crucial—typos can derail an otherwise strong application. Remember, your resume is your first impression, so make it count.

Rejection is an inevitable part of the process, but it doesn't define you. Every "no" is a stepping stone to the right opportunity. It's important to develop resilience and view each rejection as a learning experience. Maybe you need to tweak your resume or improve your interview skills. Use each experience as a chance to grow and refine your approach. Surround yourself with supportive friends or mentors who can offer encouragement and advice. Remember, the right job is out there, waiting for you to find it. Stay focused, keep learning, and trust that your efforts will pay off. The journey might be challenging, but the destination is worth it.

CRAFTING YOUR RESUME: SELLING YOURSELF

Think of your resume as your personal highlight reel—a chance to shine on paper and grab an employer's attention. Knowing someone will make a snap judgment in just a few seconds might sound intimidating, but that's precisely why your resume needs to stand out. Imagine it's the trailer for your movie; it needs to be exciting enough to make them want to see the whole film. This is your first impression, so let's make it count.

The best format for a resume depends on your level of experience and the type of job you are applying for. The **functional (skills-based) format** or a **combination format** (blending skills and work experience) are typically the best options for young adults. Which Format Should You Choose?

- **Skills-Based Format**: If you're new to the workforce or applying for roles where your skills are more relevant than your experience.
- **Combination Format**: If you have part-time jobs or volunteer experiences and want to show both your skills and your work history.

Here's a general guide to structure the resume:

1. Functional (Skills-Based) Format

Ideal for those with limited or no formal work experience, focusing on transferable skills gained through school, volunteering, hobbies, or extracurricular activities.

Structure:

1. **Contact Information**
   - Include your full name, a reliable phone number, and an email address that doesn't scream middle school (goodbye, "coolDude123"). If you have a LinkedIn profile, add that too—it shows you're serious about building your career.
2. **Objective or Summary**
   - A short, tailored statement about your goals and what you bring to the role.
     Example: *"Motivated college student with strong organizational and teamwork skills, seeking a part-time retail position to provide excellent customer service and contribute to team success."*
3. **Skills Section**
   - Group skills into categories like "Technical Skills," "Communication Skills," or "Leadership Skills."
   - Provide brief examples of how you've used these skills.
     Example:
     - *Communication Skills: Presented research findings to peers during school projects.*
     - *Technical Skills: Proficient in Microsoft Office and basic graphic design using Canva.*
4. **Education**
   - Include your school, expected graduation date, and relevant coursework or achievements (e.g., GPA if 3.5 or higher, awards, or leadership roles in school clubs).
5. **Volunteer Work, Extracurriculars, or Projects**
   - Highlight activities that demonstrate skills like teamwork, leadership, or initiative.
     Example:
     - *Organized a fundraiser for the school club, raising $1,200 for local charities.*

2. Combination Format

This format combines a skills section with a chronological listing of work or volunteer experiences. It's ideal if you have some experience (e.g., part-time jobs, internships, or volunteer roles) but still want to emphasize your skills.

Structure:

1. **Contact Information**
   - Same as above.
2. **Objective or Summary**
   - Same as above.
3. **Skills Section**
   - Include 3–5 key skills with examples.
4. **Work or Volunteer Experience** (reverse chronological order)
   - List part-time jobs, internships, or volunteer roles with job title, organization, dates, and a few bullet points detailing your responsibilities and accomplishments. Example:
     Team Member – Local Ice Cream Shop
     June 2023 – Present
     - Provided friendly customer service to over 50 customers daily.
     - Maintained cleanliness and stocked supplies efficiently.
     - Trained two new employees on store procedures.
5. **Education**
   - Same as above.

Key Tips for Formatting

- **Keep It Simple and Clean**: Use a basic font like Arial or Times New Roman, size 10–12, with consistent formatting for headings and bullet points. Avoid using graphics or flashy designs unless applying for a creative role.
- **Keep It to One Page**: A concise, one-page resume is ideal for those starting their career.
- **Use Action Verbs**: Make your bullet points impactful with verbs like "organized," "created," "led," or "assisted."
- **Quantify achievements** whenever possible (e.g., *"Increased social media engagement by 30%,"* or *"Managed a team of 5 interns"*) to showcase real impact.
- **Tailor for Each Job**: Showcase the skills and experiences that best match the specific role you're applying for, and craft a focused, job-specific objective or summary.

Your resume is your ticket to the next stage of the hiring process. Make it as polished, relevant, and engaging as possible, and you'll be one step closer to landing your dream job.

ACE YOUR JOB INTERVIEW

Stepping into a job interview can feel a bit like walking onto a stage for the first time. Your heart might race, and your hands might feel slightly clammy, but remember, you're not alone in this experience. **Preparation** is your best friend here. Before you even set foot in the interview room, take some time to **get to know the company**. Dive into their website, browse their social media, and read up on any recent news articles about them. This shows you're genuinely interested and helps you understand their values and culture. **Practice** common interview questions like, "Tell me about yourself" or "Why do you want to work here?" out loud, preferably with a friend or in front of a mirror. This helps you refine your answers and build confidence. Don't forget to **prepare a few questions** for your interviewers too. It's not just about them choosing you—you're also deciding if this is the right place for you to grow.

When it comes to **dressing for success**, think of it as a way to show respect and professionalism. Even if the company's dress code is casual, aim to dress a notch above. Business casual is usually a safe bet —think clean lines, muted colors, and nothing too flashy. Your appearance sends a message before you even say a word, so make sure it's the right one. **Pay attention to grooming** also: neat hair, clean nails, and polished shoes can make all the difference. Imagine you're meeting someone important for the first time—because you are. You want to put your best foot forward and make a lasting impression.

Interviews can be nerve-wracking, but they're also your chance to shine. **Confidence** is key, but don't let it tip into arrogance. Talk openly about your strengths, but be honest about what you're still learning. This **humility** shows self-awareness and a willingness to grow. When answering questions, take a moment to **think before**

speaking. Your answers should be concise yet clear, highlighting your skills and experiences. This approach tells the interviewer you're thoughtful and articulate. Asking insightful questions like "What does success look like in this role?" or "What's the team culture like?" shows your interest and helps you gauge if the company aligns with your values and career goals.

The interview doesn't end when you walk out the door. Follow up with a **thank-you email** within 24 hours. Keep it short but sincere. Thank them for their time, mention something specific you discussed, and reiterate your enthusiasm for the role. This simple gesture can set you apart from other candidates, showing professionalism and appreciation. It leaves a positive impression and keeps you fresh in the interviewer's mind.

NETWORKING AND BUILDING RELATIONSHIPS

Imagine entering a room buzzing with energy, where every handshake or introduction could lead to your next big opportunity. That's the magic of networking! Did you know up to 85% of jobs are filled through networking? In fact, around 70% of people land their current job thanks to the connections they've made. (Zippia. "25+ Important Networking Statistics [2023]: The Power of Connections In The Workplace" Zippia.com. Feb. 23, 2023,). It's not just about what you know—it's who you know that can open doors to internships, dream jobs, and insider advice that gets you ahead. Think of networking as your **backstage pass** to a hidden job market, where the best opportunities often get snatched up before they're even posted. To unlock this world, you've got to be proactive, strategic, and ready to make your move!

Networking events are goldmines of potential connections. Whether it's a career fair, a conference, or a casual meetup, these gatherings offer a chance to introduce yourself, ask insightful questions, and exchange contact details. Imagine chatting with someone who shares your passion and could unlock doors you didn't even know existed.

Bring business cards if you have them—they're a tangible reminder of your interaction. But the key is **follow-up**. A quick email or connecting on LinkedIn saying, "It was great meeting you, let's stay in touch," keeps the connection alive and shows you're genuinely interested in building a relationship. Maintaining these connections can be the difference between a fleeting encounter and a lasting professional friendship.

In this digital age, **online networking** is just as vital. Platforms like **LinkedIn** are your professional playground. Craft a profile that showcases your skills, experiences, and aspirations. Start following companies you're interested in and engage with their content. Connect with people in your desired industry, and don't be shy about sending a message to introduce yourself. A simple greeting and a comment about shared interests can spark a conversation. Remember, online networking is not just about collecting contacts, but about building meaningful relationships.

Building relationships goes beyond reaching out when you need something. It's about creating genuine, mutual connections. Stay in touch with people in your field, offer help when you can, and share useful information or opportunities. Think of networking as nurturing a garden. It requires time, patience, and effort. But the rewards—a robust network that supports your career development and opens up future opportunities—are worth it. **Be generous** with your knowledge and support, and you'll find that people are often willing to reciprocate. Networking is a **two-way street**; the strongest relationships are built on mutual respect and collaboration.

WORKPLACE ETIQUETTE

Stepping into your first job or internship, you might wonder how to make a solid impression. It turns out **professional behavior** is your best friend here. **Showing up on time** is more than just a courtesy; it's a sign of **respect** and **reliability**. Think of it like being the person everyone can count on. When deadlines loom, having the reputation of completing tasks as promised can set you apart. Even when the work feels tedious, bringing a positive attitude can transform the environment. Colleagues and supervisors notice and appreciate when you're **proactive** and **engaged**, even in routine tasks. After all, enthusiasm can be contagious, inspiring those around you and fostering a more enjoyable workplace.

Now, let's talk **communication**. Whether you're chatting with your boss, coworkers, or clients, how you express yourself matters. Clear, respectful communication is essential, whether in-person, via email, or over chat. Imagine your words as bridges, connecting ideas and people. Avoid using too much slang or emojis unless you're in an ultra-casual setting. While they're fun with friends, they can sometimes cloud your message in a professional context. Instead, focus on being **concise** and **polite**. When emailing, remember that tone doesn't always translate, so double-check for clarity and warmth. This approach ensures your message is understood and valued, helping you build strong professional relationships.

Office politics—it's a term that might make you cringe, but it's something you'll likely encounter. Navigating these waters means staying clear of gossip and unnecessary drama. Focus on building positive relationships with everyone, not just those in positions of power. Being known as someone who is approachable and fair can earn you respect across the board. It's about maintaining a reputation for **integrity** and **professionalism**. When conflicts arise, staying neutral and avoiding taking sides can save you from getting entangled in disputes. Remember, your goal is to contribute positively to the workplace, not to become part of its drama.

Understanding company policies is like having a map to navigate office life. Each workplace comes with its own set of rules, from dress codes to social media policies. Familiarizing yourself with these guidelines ensures you're always on the right track. Maybe there's a casual Friday dress code or restrictions on social media use during work hours. Knowing these details helps you avoid missteps and shows you respect the **company's culture** and **expectations**. When it comes to time off, understand the process for requests and approvals. This knowledge helps you plan personal time without disrupting your responsibilities. Being well-versed in company policies reflects your commitment to adapting and thriving in your new professional environment.

EXCELLING IN YOUR JOB

Once you've landed that job, it's crucial to understand what's expected of you. Dive deep into your **job description** and make sure you're clear about your **responsibilities**. If something's fuzzy, don't hesitate to ask your supervisor for clarification. This shows that you care about doing things right and are proactive about your role. It's all about getting started on the right foot and ensuring you're aligned with your team's goals. A clear understanding of your duties helps you focus on what really matters and prevents unnecessary stress down the road. Don't wait for problems to arise—being **proactive** sets the tone for a successful experience.

Time management becomes your best friend as you juggle tasks and responsibilities. Tools like calendars, to-do lists, and productivity apps help you stay organized. Break big projects into bite-sized tasks with realistic deadlines—this makes overwhelming work manageable and keeps you motivated as you check things off. But here's the key: **It's not about getting everything done—it's about getting the right things done well.** Prioritize tasks that have the biggest impact or the most pressing deadlines, and focus your energy there. This approach not only reduces stress and prevents burnout but also helps you stand out by delivering high-quality results on what truly matters. (For more strategies, review Chapter 4 on Time Management, Prioritization, and Productivity.)

Feedback isn't just something you get only during annual reviews. **Seeking feedback** regularly is a smart move. A simple question like, "How am I doing?" or "Anything I can improve on?" can open doors to valuable insights. It shows that you're committed to **personal growth** and improving your **performance**. This openness helps you identify areas for improvement and builds trust with your supervisor and colleagues. It demonstrates that you're not just there to clock in and out but are genuinely invested in contributing to the team's success. Embrace feedback as an opportunity to learn, adapt, and enhance your skills.

When challenges arise—and they will—**staying calm** is your superpower. It's easy to feel overwhelmed, but taking a step back and thinking through solutions is crucial. Before seeking help, try to brainstorm possible fixes on your own. This shows **initiative** and **problem-solving skills**, qualities that supervisors appreciate. However, if a problem feels too big to tackle alone, don't hesitate to ask for assistance. It's better to **seek guidance** than to let a small issue snowball into a major setback. By approaching challenges with a **solution-oriented mindset**, you position yourself as a valuable asset to your team, someone who actively contributes to problem-solving rather than just pointing out issues.

ACTION PLAN

Path 1: Improving in Your Current Career

1. **Set Professional Goals**:
    - Identify areas for growth and create SMART goals, like earning a certification or improving a skill.
    - Seek mentorship or shadow colleagues to expand your knowledge and network.

2. **Show Initiative**:
    - Take on new responsibilities to demonstrate leadership and adaptability.

- Meet your manager to discuss your current performance and your aspirations. Regularly communicate with your manager about your goals and contributions

Path 2: Looking for a New Job

1. **Polish Your Resume**:
    - Treat it like your personal highlight reel—showcase your skills, achievements, and impact.
    - Use action verbs and back up accomplishments with numbers (e.g., "Increased sales by 15%").
    - Keep it neat, easy to read, and visually appealing.

2. **Craft Your Application**:
    - Research companies and tailor your resume and cover letter for each role. This is more than just landing any job; it's also about finding one where you can shine.
    - Highlight how your skills align with the company's mission and the role's requirements.

3. **Stay Organized and Persistent**:
    - Set SMART goals (e.g., apply to three jobs weekly or attend two networking events monthly).
    - Remember, job-hunting is a numbers game. On average, job seekers submit 21–80 applications to land one offer (Zippia. "How Many Applications Does It Take To Get A Job? [2023]" Zippia.com. Feb. 6, 2023). Rejections are a normal part of the process, so don't get discouraged—each application brings you closer to success!

4. **Ace the Interview**:
    - Practice with mock interviews to refine your answers and body language.
    - Plan questions to ask the interviewer to show genuine interest in the role.

- Dress professionally in something that makes you feel confident.

No matter your path, career growth requires proactive steps. Whether you're aiming for a promotion or switching to your dream job, stay focused and persistent. Each experience builds the skills and resilience you need to thrive in the professional world. Keep going—you've got this!

MAKE A DIFFERENCE WITH YOUR REVIEW

Your Words Can Help Someone on Their Adulting Journey

"We make a living by what we get, but we make a life by what we give."

— WINSTON CHURCHILL

Adulting isn't easy, but the right guidance can make all the difference. Would you help someone eager to become independent, confident, and in control of their future?

My goal with **Adulting Made Simple** is to make growing up **less confusing, less stressful, and way more manageable**. But most people choose books based on reviews—that's why I need your help.

Leaving a review takes **less than a minute, costs nothing, and could change the game** for someone struggling to figure things out. Your words could:

✅ Help a young adult make smart financial decisions.
✅ Give a college student the confidence to cook real meals.
✅ Empower a first-time job seeker to ace their interview.
✅ Make adulting less overwhelming—budgeting, laundry, taxes, and more.
✅ Inspire someone to take action, knowing they're not alone.

Ready to Pay It Forward?
Scan the QR code or click here to leave a quick review: [https://www.amazon.com/review/review-your-purchases/?asin=BOOKASIN]

If you love helping others, sharing what works, and making life easier, you're my kind of person. Thank you so much!
Loren Hayes

6

COMMUNICATION, SOCIAL SKILLS, AND RELATIONSHIP BUILDING

Walking into a room full of people—potential friends, mentors, or allies—can feel overwhelming when you're unsure how to read social cues. It's like trying to decode a new language without a guide. Here's the secret: communication is your ultimate cheat code. Whether texting a crush, negotiating with a teacher, or chatting with a friend, the way you communicate shapes your interactions and relationships. It's not just about words—it's about connection, understanding, and being understood. Mastering this skill isn't just helpful; it's the key to building strong relationships, achieving your goals, and becoming the best version of yourself.

EFFECTIVE COMMUNICATION: TALKING THE TALK

Crushing it with communication is all about nailing the vibe. It's not just what you say—it's how you say it (and sometimes, what you don't say at all). Let's break it down:

- **Verbal Communication:** This is all about your words and how you deliver them—your tone, volume, and how clear you are. Think about how saying "fine" can mean anything from

"I'm great" to "I'm totally annoyed," depending on your tone. Small changes can completely flip the meaning.
- **Nonverbal Communication:** This is your silent superpower—your body language, facial expressions, gestures, and posture. For example, crossing your arms might make you seem standoffish, even if that's not your vibe. Your body often says as much (or more) than your words.
- **Written Communication:** Whether it's texts, social media posts, or emails, clarity is key. Emojis are fun but can't always save you from being misunderstood. What you write leaves a lasting impression, so make it count.

Get these layers of communication down, and you'll be able to handle pretty much any situation with confidence and connection.

Effective communication isn't just about talking; it's also about listening—really listening. **Active listening** involves more than just nodding along or saying "uh-huh" every few seconds. It's about showing you care. Your **body language** speaks volumes here: nod occasionally, lean in, and maintain eye contact to demonstrate you're engaged. Ask clarifying questions; it shows you're paying attention and want to understand better. Try saying something like, "So what you're saying is..." to **paraphrase**, which confirms your understanding and shows you're genuinely listening. And remember, let the speaker finish before you jump in. Interrupting can make people feel undervalued.

Expressing yourself clearly is another critical piece of the communication puzzle. It's about putting your thoughts and feelings into words without getting tongue-tied. Start by **thinking before you speak**—pause to gather your thoughts and avoid awkward rambling. Use "I" statements to express your feelings without blaming others. Instead of saying, "You're always late," try, "I feel frustrated when you're late." **Specificity** is critical; avoid vague statements. Instead of "You're a bad friend," say, "I was hurt when you didn't call me back." **Choose your words carefully**, and steer clear of offensive language. While you're expressing yourself, remember to practice active listening. Pay attention to the other person's response and be open to feedback.

Communication barriers are like walls that can block understanding, but they're not impossible to overcome. **Distractions** are a major culprit—smartphones, anyone? Put your phone down and really focus on the conversation. If emotions are running high, **take a break** if you're too upset to talk, and come back when you're calmer. **Misunderstandings** can also trip you up. If you're unsure what someone means, ask questions. Don't assume you know exactly what they're trying to say. Clear communication is a two-way street, requiring effort from both sides.

> Take a moment to reflect on your recent conversations. Think about a time when you felt truly understood. What made that exchange successful? Now, consider another time when communication broke down. What barriers did you face? Use this reflection to identify areas where you can improve. Write down one goal for enhancing your communication skills this week—whether it's practicing active listening, using "I" statements, or minimizing distractions. Keep track of your progress and note any changes in your interactions.

MAKING FRIENDS AND BUILDING RELATIONSHIPS

Striking up a conversation can feel like attempting a high-wire act without a net. Yet, the secret to making it look easy lies in mastering a few simple tricks. Imagine you're at a party, trying to mingle with new faces. Instead of cornering someone with questions that lead to dead ends, open the door to more meaningful conversations by **asking open-ended questions**. These questions are like keys that unlock deeper dialogue. For instance, instead of asking, "Did you like the movie?" try, "What did you think about the ending of the movie?" This approach invites the other person to share their thoughts and keeps the conversation flowing naturally. You'll often find common ground in these discussions. Perhaps you both love the same genre of music or watch the same shows. Use these shared interests as stepping stones to forge a connection. When you **add a genuine smile and a sprinkle of enthusiasm**, you become someone people are eager to chat with.

Being courteous and polite might seem old-school, but these timeless rules still carry weight. Imagine you're grabbing coffee with a friend. Saying "please" and "thank you" to the barista isn't just polite; it's a simple way to spread positivity. Holding the door open for someone, especially when their hands are full, shows consideration. **Punctuality** is another form of respect. Arriving on time signals that you value others' time as much as yours. And remember, politeness isn't reserved only for friends and family. **Treating everyone with equal respect**, regardless of their role or status, reflects well on you and sets the tone for positive interactions. **Avoid interrupting**—let others finish their thoughts before jumping in. This small act shows that you respect what they have to say.

Friendships are like plants—they need care and attention to thrive. It's not just about being there physically but showing up emotionally. Be the friend who listens, offers support, and celebrates their wins. Whether helping them through tough times or sharing in their joys, your presence matters. Even when life gets busy, small gestures like a quick text or a check-in call can make a big difference. Open and honest communication is the foundation of any strong friendship. Share your thoughts, listen to theirs, and **respect each other's boundaries**. This mutual understanding creates a safe, supportive space where you both feel valued. Mistakes will happen—no friendship is perfect. That's where **forgiveness** comes in. It's a healing act that allows you to move past hurt and rebuild trust, making the bond even stronger. Choosing to forgive doesn't just mend the relationship—it helps it grow.

Of course, friendships aren't always smooth sailing. **Disagreements and misunderstandings happen**. When they do, approach the situation with **honesty and calmness**. If you feel left out, express it without accusation, like saying, "I felt left out when I wasn't invited."

This opens the door for dialogue without putting the other person on the defensive. Listen to their side, as understanding their perspective can help resolve the issue amicably. Not every disagreement needs to escalate into a conflict. Sometimes, **agreeing to disagree** is the healthiest option. Be willing to **compromise**, as friendships often require a bit of give and take. If you're struggling to find common ground, seeking advice from a trusted adult or counselor can provide clarity and support.

Balancing friendships with other commitments can be a juggling act. School, family, and personal responsibilities all vie for your attention. It's essential to set priorities and decide what truly matters to you. **Planning ahead** can make a big difference—schedule time for friends, but also for studying, family dinners, and self-care. **Learn to say no** when your plate is full—it's okay to decline invitations if you're swamped. **Combining activities** can also help. Invite a friend to join you for a study session or a workout. This way, you're catching up while still being productive. Amidst all this, don't forget to **take care of yourself**. Getting enough sleep, eating well, and exercising are vital to maintaining your energy and focus. This balance ensures that you're present and engaged, whether with friends or tackling other responsibilities.

CONFLICT RESOLUTION: AVOIDING DRAMA

Conflict is as much a part of life as breathing. Sometimes, we clash with others over miscommunications. It's like playing a game of telephone where the original message gets lost along the way. Misunderstandings can spark disagreements, leaving both sides feeling unheard. Other times, conflict arises from different values or beliefs. You might have strong opinions about a topic, and when someone challenges those views, it can feel like a personal attack. It's natural to want others to see things from your perspective, but remember, we're all shaped by our unique experiences. Unmet expectations can also stir the pot. Maybe you expected a friend to act a certain way, but they didn't, leading to disappointment. Stress and fatigue are sneaky culprits too. When you're overwhelmed or tired, even minor annoyances can explode into full-blown arguments.

When tempers are running high, knowing how to **hit pause and cool down** is crucial. Staying calm can feel impossible in the heat of the moment, but here's a simple trick: distract your mind with a bit of math. Start with 10 + 9 + 8 + 7, and keep adding the numbers as you go down to 1. It shifts your focus away from the stress, giving your brain a break from the emotional overload. This quick mental exercise is like pressing a reset button. It not only helps you relax but also gives you a moment to collect your thoughts and approach the situation with a clearer, more level-headed perspective. Best of all, you can do it anywhere—no calculator needed!

Listening is another key element. Instead of planning your rebuttal, hear the other person out. Try understanding their viewpoint without letting your emotions cloud your judgment. **Using "I" statements** can be your best friend here. They help you express feelings without placing blame, like saying, "I felt overlooked when my ideas weren't considered," rather than, "You never listen to me." It's OK to stand up for yourself, but keep things **respectful**. Assertiveness isn't about dominating the conversation; it's about expressing yourself confidently. Sometimes, the best resolution involves compromise. It's not about winning or losing—it's about finding a middle ground where both parties feel valued.

Emotions can sometimes hijack our rational thinking during conflicts, making it essential to manage them effectively. Start by identifying what you're feeling. Are you angry, hurt, or simply frustrated? **Naming your emotions** is the first step in addressing them. **Express these feelings in a healthy way**. Whether you talk it out with a friend, jot it down in a journal, or release tension through exercise, find a method that works for you. If things get too heated, don't be afraid to call a **time-out**. Stepping away from the situation can prevent saying something you might regret. **Recognizing your trig-**

gers can also help. Maybe it's being interrupted or feeling ignored. Once you know what sets you off, you can work on managing those reactions.

Resolving a conflict doesn't stop once the argument ends. **Following up** is just as essential to ensure the issue is truly settled. If you realize you were at fault, **apologize**. A genuine "I'm sorry" can mend more than you think. Sometimes, asking, "Are we good?" a day or two later can clear the air and reassure both parties that there are no lingering hard feelings. **Reflecting** on the experience helps too. Consider what sparked the conflict and what you learned from it. This reflection can guide you in handling future disagreements more effectively. Understanding your role in the situation and how to avoid similar pitfalls in the future is an invaluable part of personal growth.

Conflicts are inevitable, but they don't have to end with drama. With the right approach, they can be opportunities for deeper understanding and stronger connections.

MANNERS MATTER: ETIQUETTE FOR COMMON SOCIAL SITUATIONS

Navigating social situations can sometimes feel like stepping into a whole new world, especially when it comes to **dining out**. Picture yourself in a nice restaurant, surrounded by clinking glasses and quiet conversations. Knowing the basics of dining etiquette can help you feel at ease. Start with the place setting—it might look complicated with all those forks, knives, and spoons, but there's a simple trick: **work from the outside in** with each course. The fork on the far left is for the salad, and the one next to it is for your entrée. The knife and spoon on the right follow the same rule. Here's a pro tip for figuring out your bread plate and drinking glasses: **think BMW—Bread, Meal, Water.** Your bread plate is on your left, and your drinking glasses are on your right. This trick can save you from awkward moments of grabbing someone else's roll or sipping from the wrong glass.

Wait until everyone is served before you start eating. It's not just polite; it's a moment to pause and enjoy the company. **Chew with your mouth closed** and avoid slurping your soup. Loud eating noises can be distracting, and you want your dining companions to focus on your brilliant conversation—not your table manners! **Phones should stay off the table**, especially in formal settings. If you absolutely need to check something, excuse yourself from the table. And don't forget to **say "please" and "thank you"** to the waitstaff. They're working hard to make your experience enjoyable.

When it comes to **parties**, timing is important. Show up about 10 to 15 minutes after the start time. Arriving too early can catch your host off guard while being too late might make you miss out on the fun. If you're heading to a potluck or BYOB event, don't be that person who shows up empty-handed. **Ask your host what you can bring** or opt for something easy like chips or drinks. It's a small gesture that shows your appreciation for being invited. Plus, it's a great conversation starter. "Hey, who brought the awesome guacamole?" could lead to meeting someone new.

Meeting parents or professionals can be nerve-wracking, but remember, **first impressions matter**. Dress appropriately for the situation. You don't need to wear a suit, but showing up in pajamas isn't the best idea either. Consider the setting—casual, business casual, or formal—and dress accordingly. When you walk in, **be respectful but relaxed**. Greet them with a genuine smile and a firm handshake. Don't overthink it. **A handshake is about connecting**, not seeing who has the strongest grip. Look them in the eyes and hold the handshake for about two to three seconds. Be aware that not all cultures value handshakes. In some places, a nod or bow might be more fitting. Being mindful of these nuances shows respect for different customs.

Knowing how to make **proper introductions** is a key social skill that helps you show respect, build connections, and make a positive impression in any setting. In social or professional settings, introductions follow a simple rule: **introduce the less important person to the more important person first.** Here are some quick examples:

- **Social Settings**

Introduce the younger or less prominent person to the older or more prominent person.

"Grandma, this is my friend Sarah. Sarah, this is my grandmother, Mrs. Thompson."

- **Professional Settings**

Introduce a junior colleague to a senior or higher-ranking individual.

"Mr. Lopez, this is Emily, our new intern. Emily, this is Mr. Lopez, our company's director."

- **Mixed Settings**

Prioritize formal roles over personal relationships.

"Mayor Davis, this is my cousin Jake. Jake, this is Mayor Davis."

- **Group Settings**

Start with the most prominent person, then introduce others.

"Professor Chen, this is our project team: Alex, Taylor, and Jordan."

Keep it brief and respectful, and you'll always make a great impression.

ACTION PLAN

You've got the tools; now it's time to implement them.

1. **Practice Communication**:

   - Next time you hang out with a friend, actively practice good communication—listen without interrupting, ask thoughtful questions, and show genuine interest in their stories.
   - Address small conflicts with a friend or housemate instead of ignoring them—talk it out calmly, be honest about your feelings, and work toward a solution. Stronger relationships come from clear, open communication.

2. **Expand Your Social Circle**:

   - Take small steps to meet new people—strike up a conversation in line, before class, or at an event.
   - Use simple openers like "Hey, how's your day going?" to start a conversation—you never know where it might lead!
   - Challenge yourself to initiate one new interaction this week to build confidence and expand your social network.

3. **Brush Up on Social Etiquette**:

   - Prepare for social events by considering the setting, dressing appropriately, and thinking about how you'll introduce yourself.
   - Practice small gestures like making eye contact, shaking hands, and saying "thank you" to create positive impressions.

- Be aware of your surroundings—show respect in group settings by listening, contributing thoughtfully, and being considerate of others.

4. **Strengthen Relationships**:

- Make time to connect—send a quick text, plan a coffee meetup, or check in with a friend or family member.
- Expand your perspective by engaging with people from different backgrounds and experiences.
- Build meaningful connections—strong relationships not only improve your personal life but can open doors in your career and future opportunities.

Putting these strategies into practice enhances your relationships and boosts your self-esteem. You'll find that the more you engage with others, the more you learn about different perspectives, which is a priceless skill in both personal and professional settings. These interactions build your network, which can open doors to opportunities you hadn't imagined. Remember, life is about connections—making them, nurturing them, and growing from them. As you become more comfortable, you'll naturally gravitate toward more meaningful and fulfilling interactions. So, go ahead and make the most of the relationships in your life. They're not just a part of your journey; they are what make it worthwhile.

7

DIGITAL LITERACY AND ONLINE SAFETY

MANAGING YOUR SOCIAL MEDIA PRESENCE: CURATING YOUR ONLINE BRAND

Scrolling through your Instagram feed, liking photos, watching TikToks, and posting memes probably feels like just another part of your day. But have you ever stopped to think about the digital footprint you're leaving behind? In today's world, managing your online presence is as crucial as choosing what clothes to wear for an important event. Whether you're sharing a funny video or documenting a day out, everything you post contributes to your **personal brand**. And just like you wouldn't wear pajamas to a job interview, you want to make sure that what you share online reflects your best version of yourself. This digital age makes it easy to connect with others, but it also means your online reputation can follow you around like a shadow.

Your online presence can open or close doors, impacting your social life, college applications, and even job prospects. Imagine someone considering you for an opportunity and checking out your social media. What would they find? Would your posts make you seem fun and engaging, or could they raise eyebrows? It's essential to consider how your online activity reflects on you. Before posting, ask yourself, "Would I want my grandma to see this?" If the answer is no, maybe hit pause. A **positive online reputation** can enhance your chances in life, helping build relationships and paving the way for future success. Social media is a powerful tool that can showcase your talents, interests, and achievements, so use it wisely to create a brand that highlights your best attributes.

Privacy is another crucial piece of the puzzle. Let's be honest—most of us skip the fine print. But taking a moment to adjust your privacy settings on Instagram, TikTok, and other platforms can protect you in big ways. You don't have to share everything with everyone. Set your accounts to private and control who sees your content! For example, only approved followers on Instagram should see your posts if you opt for a private account. This way, you maintain control over your audience, limiting it to those you trust. Adjusting privacy settings can protect you from unwanted attention and keep your personal life just that—personal.

Just because you can post something doesn't mean you should. Oversharing can backfire, leading to regrets later on. Before hitting "share," think about the long-term impact. Could this post embarrass you in the future or hurt someone else? If there's any doubt, it's better to keep it to yourself. For example, think twice before posting sensitive personal details like your school, workplace, or daily routines. While they might seem harmless, these details can be misused by someone with bad intentions, leaving you vulnerable to identity theft, stalking, or other risks. **Protecting your privacy** ensures your **safety** and peace of mind.

Your online presence should reflect the best version of you. Share achievements, creative projects, or passions like photography, sports, or music to craft a positive digital persona. Keep in mind that every post leaves a digital trail, even if deleted. Colleges, employers, and others could uncover old content, so think about the **legacy** you're creating. Your **digital footprint** tells your story—make it one you're proud of.

> **Online Persona Checklist**
> - **Review Your Profiles**: Ensure your profiles reflect who you are. Update bios and delete old posts that don't match your current self.
> - **Adjust Privacy Settings**: Make accounts private and limit who can see your posts.
> - **Share Wisely**: Post content that aligns with your goals and values. Avoid oversharing personal details.
> - **Monitor Your Digital Footprint**: Search your name online to see what comes up and adjust your privacy settings as needed.

RECOGNIZING AND AVOIDING ONLINE THREATS: STAYING SAFE ONLINE

You're scrolling through your emails when an urgent subject line warns about a compromised account. Panic sets in, and you're tempted to click the link. **Stop!** This could be a **phishing scam**, a trick designed to  steal your sensitive information—like passwords, credit card numbers, or Social Security details—for fraud or identity theft. These scams often impersonate trusted banks or services but include subtle red flags like spelling errors, strange links, or requests for private information that legitimate companies would never ask for. If something feels off, **trust your instincts—don't click.** When in doubt, go to the company's official website or contact them directly to confirm if the message is real.

Another common online threat is **fake profiles**. These digital chameleons blend in, but they're full of red flags. For example, receiving a friend request from someone with no followers and a blank profile should raise immediate suspicion. These profiles often aim to scam you, steal personal information, or worse. Always be cautious—if a profile feels off, it's safer to ignore or block it. Vet requests carefully and trust your instincts.

Hacking is a real threat, not just a movie plot. Hackers can access your accounts, steal personal information, or lock you out of your own devices. That's why strong, unique passwords are essential—they're the keys to your digital kingdom. Avoid simple, easy-to-guess passwords like "123456" or "password." Instead, use a mix of letters, numbers, and symbols with at least 8 characters. Since these passwords can be hard to remember, a **password manager** like **Bitwarden** can help by securely storing and generating strong passwords for you.

Cyberbullying is another threat lurking online, especially on social media platforms. It can be as subtle as a snide comment or as overt as a full-blown online attack. The anonymity of the internet can bring out the worst in some people, and it's important to know how to handle these situations. Don't engage with bullies; instead, report them to the platform and reach out to someone you trust for support. Remember, nobody deserves to feel unsafe online. You can take steps to block or mute individuals who bring negativity to your digital space.

Protecting yourself online is about being **vigilant** and **proactive**. Be mindful of the information you share and with whom you share it. Avoid clicking on unfamiliar links, especially if they come from unknown sources. Keep your personal information, like your address or phone number, private. It's easy to let your guard down when you're in the comfort of your home, scrolling through your feeds. But staying alert and informed is key to navigating the digital world safely.

> **Checklist for Online Safety**
> - **Strong Passwords**: Use a mix of letters, numbers, and symbols. Avoid common phrases.
> - **Password Manager**: Consider using Bitwarden to keep track of your passwords.
> - **Be Skeptical**: If something seems too good to be true, it probably is.
> - **Verify Links**: Hover over links to see where they lead before clicking.
> - **Report Suspicious Activity**: Notify the platform of cyberbullying or fake profiles.

DON'T BE *THAT* PERSON: MASTERING ONLINE ETIQUETTE

Online etiquette starts with the most important principle: **treat others with respect**. Just because you're behind a screen doesn't mean your words don't have an impact. If you wouldn't say something to someone's face, it's best not to say it online. It's easy to get caught up in the anonymity of the internet, but that doesn't excuse rude comments, trolling, or unnecessary fights. Trolls—people who post inflammatory or disruptive comments just to provoke reactions—thrive on attention. Don't feed into their behavior. Ignore them, report harassment, and help create a positive space where everyone feels respected.

Netiquette, or online etiquette, is another essential part of respectful online behavior. Typing in all caps is like shouting—it's uncomfortable for others. **Basic spelling and grammar** can go a long way in making your message clear and easy to understand. A little **proofreading** before you post helps avoid confusion and shows you care about what you're saying. Ask yourself if your words are kind, helpful, and contribute to the conversation. If they don't, it's better to stay silent. Your words should be like seeds—plant something positive and let it grow.

Harassment and **trolling** can have serious consequences on someone's mental health, so it's crucial to take action if you see it happening. Most platforms allow you to report such behavior, and doing so helps make the digital world safer. Remember, trolls feed on attention, so the less you engage with them, the less power they have.

Proper etiquette matters when it comes to **videoconferencing**, too. Be punctual, mute your microphone when you're not speaking, and make sure your background is appropriate. If your setting isn't ideal—like a messy room or a busy café—consider using a virtual background or a blurred effect to keep the focus on you. Good lighting and eye contact with the camera create a more professional, engaging experience. Just as you wouldn't interrupt someone in a face-to-face meeting, be mindful of others' speaking time and avoid distractions during calls. These habits help maintain respect and clarity, ensuring a positive virtual interaction.

Ultimately, your actions online shape the communities you're a part of. Be mindful of how your words and behaviors impact others, and remember that there's a real person on the other side of the screen. The internet is a vast space with room for everyone, and by following these guidelines, we can help make it a welcoming and respectful place for all.

ONLINE DATING SAFETY

Navigating the world of online dating can be exciting, yet it demands a good dose of caution. Meeting new people and exploring potential connections is thrilling, but **safety should always be your top priority**. Imagine this: you've matched with someone who seems interesting, and you're gearing up for that first meetup. Always pick a public place, like a busy coffee shop or a bustling park. These spots offer safety in numbers, and having people around can ease any first-date jitters. Let a friend or family member know your plans, including who you're meeting and where; share your location using your phone's GPS feature if possible. It's like having a buddy system, even if you're technically alone.

When you're chatting online, it's easy to feel comfortable and share a lot but pace yourself. Keep personal details—like where you live, work, or study—under wraps until you genuinely trust the person. Over time, you might feel more at ease sharing, but in the beginning, less is more. **Video chatting before meeting up** is a smart move. It's a chance to verify that the person you're speaking with looks and acts like their profile suggests. It's about building trust and ensuring that both of you are on the same page. Think of it as a preliminary face-to-face meeting but with the comfort of being in your own space.

Red flags are your internal alarm system. If your match is rushing things, being secretive, or making you uncomfortable, it's crucial to trust your instincts. Whether it's something subtle, like avoiding video calls, or more obvious, like asking for money, listen to your gut. It's always better to slow things down or end the conversation if something doesn't feel right. If someone crosses boundaries or behaves inappropriately, most dating apps have tools to report such behavior. Reporting helps protect yourself and others, ensuring the platform remains a safe, respectful space for everyone.

Online dating should be fun, but it's also about staying smart and safe. By taking simple precautions, you can explore new connections confidently. Remember, your safety and comfort are paramount. There's no rush, and taking things at your own pace is perfectly okay. Embrace the process, and don't hesitate to lean on friends and family for support and advice. Whether it's sharing your excitement over a promising new match or seeking guidance when something feels off, having a support system can make the online dating experience more enriching.

YOUR ONLINE ACTIONS MATTER: BE A RESPONSIBLE DIGITAL CITIZEN

Being a digital citizen isn't just about having access to the internet; it's about using that access responsibly. Think of it as being a good neighbor but in the online world. This means **respecting others,**

using technology ethically, and protecting your data. The internet can be a wild place, full of **information and misinformation**. It's your job to sift through it thoughtfully. Before you hit share on that shocking headline, do a quick **fact-check**. The last thing you want is to spread fake news that misleads others or causes unnecessary panic. Being informed helps you use your platform to make a positive impact, whether by sharing helpful resources or raising awareness about important issues.

Social media offers a megaphone for causes that matter to you. **Online activism** is a powerful way to contribute to change. It allows you to participate in movements that align with your values and beliefs. You've probably seen hashtags like #BlackLivesMatter or #FridaysForFuture trending on platforms like Twitter or Instagram. These movements have gained momentum thanks to the voices of people like you. But it's crucial to approach online activism with a well-informed mind. Dive into the issues, understand the context, and think critically about the information you share. This ensures your contributions are **meaningful and constructive** rather than just noise.

Digital literacy is essential for being a responsible digital citizen and confidently navigating the internet. It involves understanding how websites, apps, and social media work and being able to spot fake news, ads disguised as articles, and suspicious websites. To determine **credibility**, check the source—reliable outlets have a track record of accuracy—and verify information with multiple sources or fact-checking websites. Be wary of sensational headlines. Ads often have promotional language and lack unbiased content, so look for clear labeling of sponsored material. Suspicious websites may have poor design, pop-ups, spelling errors, or unsecured URLs. By developing digital literacy, you become a savvy consumer, able to avoid pitfalls and educate others on how to safely navigate the digital world.

Consider your digital actions as a ripple effect—what you do online impacts not only you but also others. By being a responsible digital citizen, you help create a positive and respectful online environment. Your digital footprint should reflect your values and the change you want to see in the world. Whether you're supporting a cause, sharing helpful content, or simply being kind in your interactions, every action matters. As you navigate the digital world, remember the power you have to shape it for the better.

ACTION PLAN

1. **Curate Your Online Brand:**

- Review your social media profiles and remove posts or tags that no longer represent you or might raise flags with future employers.
- Share content that reflects your values, interests, and goals—your online presence is your personal brand, so make it authentic.

2. **Lock Down Your Privacy Settings:**

- Privacy is power! Set your accounts to "friends only," enable two-factor authentication, and keep tabs on who's viewing your content.
- Be selective about friend requests, and don't let strangers snoop around your life—it's like leaving your front door open to anyone.

3. **Stay Safe Online:**

- Watch out for scams like phishing emails, fake profiles, and "too good to be true" deals. If something feels off, trust your instincts—don't click or respond.
- Use strong passwords and never reuse them across different accounts. A password manager such as Bitwarden can securely store and generate complex passwords for you, so you don't have to remember them all.
- Enable two-factor authentication (2FA) for extra security—this adds another layer of protection beyond just a password.
- Be cautious with personal information—avoid sharing details like your location, phone number, or financial info with strangers online.

4. **Practice Online Etiquette:**

- Be respectful and mindful of your tone when communicating online.
- Think before you comment or post, and ask yourself: "Would I say this face-to-face?" Once something is online, it's hard to take back.

5. **Stay Safe While Dating Online:**

- Stick to reputable dating apps, and verify profiles before engaging. Be cautious about what you share with matches.
- First dates? Meet in public and tell a friend your plans—your safety comes first.

6. **Be a Digital Role Model:**

- Share reliable info, give proper credit, and squash misinformation when you see it.

- Use your platform for good—spread positivity and stand up against online hate.

The digital world can be a wild place, but with a bit of effort, you can turn it into a space that's safe, fun, and truly yours. With these steps, you can navigate the digital world with confidence, protect your personal space, and create a meaningful online presence that reflects the real you.

8

RENTING 101

FINDING YOUR PERFECT PAD

Imagine stepping into your first apartment, a space that's entirely yours to decorate, relax, and call home. It's a thrilling thought, right? But before you get too carried away with Pinterest boards and IKEA catalogs, first, let's find your perfect pad. The renting journey can be both exciting and daunting, especially when navigating the complexities of budgets, preferences, and paperwork. But don't worry —like any great adventure, it starts with a solid plan.

The first stop on this journey is setting a realistic **budget**. It's crucial to figure out how much rent you can comfortably afford without sacrificing your other needs. A good rule of thumb is to allocate no more than 30% of your gross income to rent. This helps ensure you have enough left over for essentials like food, transportation, and other living expenses. Speaking of which, don't forget about utilities. Internet, electricity, water, and garbage services often fall outside of rent and can sneak up on you if you're not careful. Depending on where you live, some of these costs might be covered by your landlord, but it's vital to clarify this upfront. If living solo stretches your budget too thin, consider teaming up with friends or finding a roommate to share the costs. This can ease financial pressure and make the experience more enjoyable.

Next, think about what you truly **want** in your new home. Is proximity to work or school a must, or are you okay with a longer commute in exchange for a quieter neighborhood? How much space do you **need**? Maybe a cozy studio will do, or perhaps you crave the extra room of a one-bedroom. Amenities can also play a big role in your decision. An in-unit washer and dryer, parking, or a gym might be non-negotiable for you. Make a list of your **priorities** and decide what you're willing to compromise on. This will help streamline your search and prevent you from getting sidetracked by places that don't meet your needs.

Once you've nailed down your budget and wishlist, it's time to start **hunting** for that perfect place. There are plenty of ways to find potential apartments. Online listings are a great start—websites like Zillow, Apartments.com, or Craigslist can give you a sense of what's available in your area and at what price. Don't overlook local resources, though. Community boards, word of mouth, and neighborhood visits can uncover hidden gems not listed online.

When you find a place that catches your eye, contact the property manager to schedule a **viewing**. The viewing tour is your chance to check for damages and broken items like faulty appliances, broken locks, water stains, mold or mildew, and leaky plumbing. Take photos during your visit. It's easy to forget details when viewing multiple places, so snapping photos can help you compare them later and remember specific features or issues. And make sure to check out the neighborhood. Try to visit the area at different times—morning, afternoon, and evening—to get a sense of the noise levels, safety, and general vibe. Don't be shy about asking questions regarding lease terms, included utilities and maintenance responsibilities.

Comparing different apartments can feel overwhelming, but a simple pros and cons list can work wonders. Consider the total monthly costs, including rent and utilities, and consider how each place fits your long-term goals. Will this apartment suit your needs a year from now, or is it just a stopgap? Once you've found a place that ticks most of your boxes, it's time to gather the necessary **paperwork**. Landlords typically want proof of income—like pay stubs or bank statements—and a valid ID. Be ready for a **credit check** or to provide **references**, as these are common steps in the application process.

> Create your apartment wishlist. List your must-haves, nice-to-haves, and deal-breakers. This exercise will help clarify what you're really looking for and guide your search. Keep this list handy when viewing potential apartments to ensure you're evaluating them based on what truly matters to you.

UNDERSTANDING LEASE AGREEMENTS. READ BEFORE YOU SIGN

Stepping into the world of renting means facing a stack of paperwork, and right at the top is the all-important **lease agreement**. This document isn't just a formality; it's the rulebook for your new home. Understanding the terms inside can save you headaches down the road. A lease outlines your legal obligations, such as paying rent on time and maintaining the property. It also spells out your rights, like having a safe living environment. Missing a critical detail could mean unexpected fees or even legal trouble. So, take your time reading it, and don't hesitate to ask your landlord for clarification on anything that seems fuzzy.

Focus on the key components of the lease. Start with **rent details**: know the amount due each month, the due date, and how to pay—whether online, by check, or through a portal. **Security deposits** are next. You'll pay this upfront, usually equal to one or two months' rent, as a safety net for your landlord in case of damages. Make sure you understand the conditions for getting this deposit back. The **lease term** is crucial too; it tells you how long you're committed—typically six months to a year. Be aware of notice periods for renewal or termination so you're never caught off guard. Then, **maintenance responsibilities** outline what you need to fix and what falls to the landlord—knowing who handles what can prevent disputes and ensure timely repairs. Always clarify these points if you're unsure.

Leases often include clauses with implications you should understand. **Early termination** clauses explain what happens if you need to break the lease early. There might be **penalties**, so weigh your options carefully. **Subletting** clauses let you know if you can rent out your place to someone else, which could be handy if you need to leave temporarily. **Pet policies** are also standard, detailing any restrictions, deposits, or fees if you plan to have a furry friend. These clauses can affect your living situation, so it's essential to know them inside and out.

If you come across lease terms that don't fully suit your needs, keep in mind that they can often be negotiated. For example, if the apartment has been on the market for a while or requires some repairs, you could ask for a rent reduction. If you want a shorter commitment, you might request more flexible lease terms. You could also inquire about adding amenities, like upgraded appliances or parking spaces, to make the deal more appealing. While **negotiating** may seem intimidating, approaching it respectfully and with clear reasoning could make a landlord more willing to work with you than you might think.

ROOMMATE AGREEMENTS: SETTING BOUNDARIES AND EXPECTATIONS

Living with roommates can be an adventure, filled with late-night chats, shared meals, and the occasional squabble over the last slice of pizza. But to keep things running smoothly, having a roommate agreement is a lifesaver. It's not just a piece of paper; it's a roadmap for cohabitation. By **setting clear expectations and responsibilities** from the get-go, you can prevent many headaches. An agreement outlines everything from who pays what bills to how chores are divided. This clarity helps avoid misunderstandings and sets the stage for a harmonious living arrangement. Plus, it offers **legal protection** in case disputes arise. If you're leasing together, make sure each person signs their own lease agreement to ensure **fairness and shared responsibility**.

When drafting a roommate agreement, focus on the hot spots that often lead to conflict. First up is **rent and utilities**—how will these costs be divided, and who is responsible for making payments? Next, tackle **household chores**. Assign tasks like vacuuming, taking out the trash, and cleaning shared spaces. This keeps the apartment tidy and ensures that everyone pitches in. Discuss **guidelines for shared spaces** like the kitchen and living room to maintain a comfortable environment for all. **Guest policies** are another crucial topic—set rules for having friends over and overnight guests so everyone knows what to expect. These terms don't have to be formal, but they should be clear enough to guide daily living.

To keep the peace, **regular check-ins** with your roommates are essential. Schedule monthly meetings to discuss any issues or changes in your living situation. This practice encourages open communication and nips potential problems in the bud. When conflicts do arise, address them directly and calmly. Use techniques like active listening and compromise to find solutions that work for everyone. Respecting each other's boundaries is crucial—everyone needs space and privacy. Encourage a culture of mutual respect and consideration where everyone feels valued and heard. Establish **house rules** that reflect your shared values and lifestyle, whether it's about noise levels, cleaning schedules, or quiet hours. Flexibility and compromise are key. Life happens and sometimes plans change. Being willing to adapt and accommodate each other's needs strengthens the household dynamic and fosters a supportive environment.

MOVING IN AND OUT

Moving into a new place is like starting a fresh chapter, full of potential and excitement. But before you get those keys and start envisioning your new setup, it's crucial to do a thorough **walkthrough**. Think of this as your chance to play detective. Check for existing damage like scratches on the floor, stains on the walls, or anything that doesn't seem right. Take photos and write down notes about these issues. It might feel like a hassle, but documenting everything ensures you aren't blamed for damages that were there before you moved in. This step is about protecting yourself and ensuring you get that security deposit back when it's time to move out.

Speaking of **utilities**, it's important to clarify what's included in your rent. Utilities like **electricity, gas, water, and internet** are often not covered, so you'll need to set up accounts with local providers before moving in. This way, when you unlock that front door for the first time, you'll have power, heat, and water all setup and ready to go. Trust me, there's nothing worse than moving into a dark apartment with no heat in the middle of winter because you forgot to arrange your utilities. A little foresight and planning can go a long way in ensuring a smooth, stress-free transition.

The **security deposit** is like a financial safety net for your landlord, covering any potential damage or unpaid rent. To get it back, you need to keep the place in good condition and follow the **move-out instructions** to the letter. This usually means leaving the apartment as clean as you found it and fixing any minor damages you might have caused. Some landlords might even ask for a final walkthrough to make sure everything is in tip-top shape. Keeping the property tidy and addressing any wear and tear before you leave boosts your chances of a full refund.

As you approach the end of your lease, it's crucial to know how much **notice** you need to give—typically 30 to 60 days. Mark this date in your calendar to avoid any late penalties or misunderstandings. Cleaning is your ally when it's time to pack up and go. From scrubbing floors to wiping down countertops, a clean apartment leaves a good impression and helps ensure you meet the landlord's standards. Fixing minor damage, like a scuffed wall or a loose doorknob, shows responsibility and can prevent any deductions from your deposit. Landlords appreciate tenants who leave the place as they found it, making the moving-out process smoother for everyone involved.

BEING A GOOD TENANT

Navigating the world of renting can feel like balancing on a tightrope, but being a good tenant isn't rocket science. It starts with **paying your rent on time**. Consistently meeting your rent deadline avoids late fees and builds a solid reputation with your landlord. Setting up reminders or automating payments can be a lifesaver if you tend to be forgetful. This kind of reliability shows you're responsible and trustworthy, which can be a huge plus if you need a reference in the future. Plus, no one wants the stress of scrambling to gather rent money at the last minute.

Caring for your space is another key aspect of being a good tenant. Treat your rented home as if it's your own. Keep it clean, and tackle small maintenance tasks like changing light bulbs or unclogging drains. These little actions not only maintain the property but also make it a more pleasant place to live. If a problem arises that's beyond your control—like a leaky faucet or a broken heater—report it to your landlord promptly. Quick communication can prevent small issues from turning into bigger problems, saving everyone time and stress. Remember, landlords appreciate tenants who are proactive in maintaining their property.

Communication is the glue that holds any tenant-landlord relationship together. If something's amiss, whether it's a maintenance request or a concern about your lease, don't hesitate to reach out. Clear, respectful communication helps avoid misunderstandings and ensures issues are resolved quickly. Keeping an open line of dialogue demonstrates that you're cooperative and considerate, qualities that make for a harmonious renting experience. Building a positive relationship with your landlord can also make it easier to negotiate lease renewals or request improvements to the property.

Being a good neighbor is just as important as being a good tenant. Respecting building rules and neighborhood norms goes a long way. Keep your noise levels in check, especially during late hours, and follow trash and recycling protocols to keep communal areas tidy. Be mindful of shared spaces, whether it's a laundry room or a parking area. Simple acts like these create a positive environment not only for you but for everyone living around you. Strong relationships with your neighbors can make your living situation much more enjoyable and even provide a support network in times of need.

DON'T GET CAUGHT OFF GUARD: PROTECT YOUR BELONGINGS & KNOW YOUR RIGHTS

When you're settling into a new place, one thing that often slips under the radar is **renter's insurance**. Think of it as a protective bubble around your personal belongings. Imagine your neighbor accidentally overflows their bathtub, and water seeps into your apartment, ruining your laptop and that comfy couch you just bought. Without renter's insurance, you're on the hook for replacing those items. But with it, you're covered, and you won't have to dip into your savings to get back on track. It's typically affordable, with many policies costing less than a Netflix subscription each month, offering peace of mind without breaking the bank. Check with multiple providers to find the best rate and coverage that suits your needs. This small monthly fee can save you from major financial headaches in the future, protecting against theft, damage, and even some personal liability situations.

> **Renter's Insurance Providers:**
> Here's a quick list of popular renter's insurance providers to get you started on your search: Amica, Allstate, Lemonade, and State Farm. Compare their offerings and see what fits your needs best. Each offers different packages and coverages, so be sure to read the fine print and ask questions. Remember, investing a little time in understanding your options now can save you a lot of hassle down the line.

Understanding **local tenant laws** is essential when renting. Each state has rules that govern tenant-landlord relationships. For instance, some states have specific guidelines about how much landlords can charge for late fees or how quickly they must respond to maintenance requests. Knowing these laws helps protect your rights and ensures you're meeting your responsibilities. Many local government websites offer easy-to-understand resources, and tenant rights organizations can provide support if needed. Being informed about tenant laws lays the groundwork for a smooth, stress-free renting experience.

ACTION PLAN

1. **Get Ready and Find Your Perfect Pad**:

   - **Documents**: Be prepared! Gather proof of income, your ID, references, and past landlord or employer contacts—it'll give you a competitive edge.
   - **Budget Smart**: Plan for upfront costs like first month's rent, a security deposit, and moving expenses. Don't forget essentials like furniture and household items—check thrift stores or online marketplaces for deals.
   - **Search Fast and Smart**: Make a list of places that fit your vibe, budget, and needs. Use apps, act fast, and follow up with landlords to show you're serious. Good spots go fast, so be ready to apply on the spot!
   - **Lease Agreements**: Don't rush—read every word before signing. Check for rent terms, fees, pet policies, and subletting rules. If it's confusing, ask questions.

2. **Roommate Rules = Peace of Mind**:

   - Talk early about splitting bills, chores, and guest policies.

- Put agreements in writing to avoid misunderstandings and awkward arguments later—future you will thank you.

3. **Moving In and Out Like a Pro**:

- **Moving In**: Set up utilities (electricity, internet, water) before move-in day. Pack smart with a checklist and snap photos of the space to protect your deposit.
- **Moving Out**: Clean like a boss, fix small damage, and follow the landlord's checklist to ensure your deposit comes back to you.

4. **Be a Good Tenant**:

- Pay rent on time—set reminders if needed. Communicate with your landlord, follow property rules, and respect your neighbors.
- Got a problem? Report maintenance issues ASAP. A happy landlord = a stress-free rental life.

5. **Protect Yourself**:

- Get renters insurance —it's cheap and will save your stuff if disaster strikes.
- Know your local tenant rights so you're ready to handle any tricky situation.

With a solid plan and a little hustle, you'll go from apartment-hunting newbie to renting master in no time. Your dream space is waiting—go claim it! And who knows? If you've been saving wisely, you might even be on your way to homeownership sooner than you think. Every smart financial move you make now brings you one step closer to that ultimate goal!

9

HOUSEHOLD MANAGEMENT MASTERY

Walking into your space and instantly feeling at ease is one of the best parts of independent living. A place where everything has its spot, your bed feels like a cozy retreat, and the kitchen isn't in a constant state of chaos. Sounds ideal, right? But creating this kind of environment isn't just about looks—it's about designing a space that helps you recharge, stay organized, and feel in control. Living on your own comes with both challenges and rewards, and mastering your household goes beyond tidying up. It's about setting up a home that supports your lifestyle, saves you time, and even clears mental clutter. When your space works for you, everything else in life feels just a little more manageable.

Managing a household means finding a balance between daily upkeep and making your space truly yours. You don't need to become a cleaning expert overnight. Instead, focus on **developing routines that fit into your current lifestyle**. Maybe it's setting aside some time each day for a quick tidy-up or dedicating a weekend morning to more intense cleaning. The key is consistency. A little effort every day can prevent messes from piling up and turning into overwhelming tasks. It's like building any habit—it takes time, but once it's part of your routine, it becomes second nature.

Beyond cleaning, household management involves understanding how to **use your resources wisely**. This includes everything from budgeting your household expenses to knowing how to tackle minor home repairs. Think of it this way: if you can fix a leaky faucet or change a lightbulb, you save money and the hassle of scheduling a repair. Knowing how to read your utility bills and identifying peak usage times can also help you cut down on unnecessary costs. It's about becoming self-reliant and resourceful, skills that will serve you well throughout life.

Safety is also a crucial part of managing a home. Simple habits like locking doors and windows and knowing where your emergency contacts are can greatly enhance your peace of mind. Being prepared for emergencies, such as having a first aid kit and knowing how to handle power outages or minor injuries, is essential. It's also important to understand how to use household tools and appliances safely. Safety isn't just about tidiness—it's about fostering a secure and efficient living environment where you can thrive.

CLEANING AND MAINTENANCE: KEEPING YOUR SPACE TIDY WITH MINIMAL EFFORT

Keeping your living space clean isn't just about impressing your friends or avoiding the dreaded call from your parents. A clean home brings real benefits. It reduces allergens and bacteria, making it a healthier place to live. Think about it: fewer dust bunnies mean fewer sneezes, and a germ-free kitchen means fewer colds. Plus, a tidy space helps clear your mind. You're less likely to feel overwhelmed when everything is in its place. Imagine walking into a clutter-free room after a long day. It's like a breath of fresh air for your brain, giving you the mental clarity to focus on what matters.

> Take a moment to look around your space. Pick one room and spend ten minutes tidying it up. Set a timer and focus on putting everything back in its place. You'll be amazed at how much you can accomplish in a very short time. This quick reset is a great way to start building a habit of keeping your space organized without feeling overwhelmed. Once you see the impact of a simple tidy-up, you might find yourself more motivated to tackle other areas of your home.

Creating a **simple cleaning routine** can make a world of difference. Start with the basics: clean up spills as soon as they happen to prevent stains and sticky surfaces. Make your bed each morning for an instant sense of accomplishment. Wash dishes after every meal or at least by the end of the day to keep your kitchen clean and ready for action. Wipe down counters and surfaces regularly with a microfiber cloth and all-purpose cleaner to keep germs at bay. Weekly or bi-weekly, tackle tasks like vacuuming, sweeping, mopping, and cleaning the bathroom. Don't forget laundry during this time. And once a month, give your fridge a good cleanout. It might sound like a lot, but breaking it down makes it all manageable.

To tackle household tasks, you'll need a few **essential tools**:

- Start with an **all-purpose cleaner**—store-bought or homemade with vinegar, baking soda, and lemon—for most surfaces. **Dish soap** works wonders on dishes, cookware, and greasy messes.
- **Sponges** and **rubber gloves** protect your hands while scrubbing, and **microfiber cloths** are perfect for surfaces and controlling bacteria. Keep **paper towels or rags** on hand for quick clean-ups.
- For floors, **a broom and dustpan** handle dirt, while a **spray mop with washable pads** makes mopping simple. A **vacuum** is a must for carpets and rugs.
- In the bathroom, **a toilet brush and cleaner** are essentials, along with scrub brushes for stubborn stains.

- Finally, stock the right **soap for your laundry** needs to keep your clothes fresh and clean.

Knowing **what to clean and when** is half the battle. **In the kitchen**, toss food scraps in the compost or garbage and wash dishes regularly. Replace dish towels weekly. Wipe down counters and surfaces every day, and clean up spills immediately. **In the bathroom**, use a dedicated dish sponge for the sink, shower, and tub. Scrub away mold and mildew, and wipe mirrors and fixtures. Replace towels and bath rugs weekly or bi-weekly. **In the bedroom**, make your bed daily, put dirty clothes in the hamper, and dust surfaces. Replace and wash your sheets every two weeks. Finally, **living spaces** need daily tidying, with weekly vacuuming or sweeping.

LAUNDRY 101

Laundry might seem like a never-ending task, but mastering the basics makes it a lot easier. Let's start with fabric types. **Natural fabrics** like cotton, linen, wool, and silk require specific care. Cotton is easygoing, but linen, wool, and silk need special handling and may bleed colors. **Synthetic fabrics** like polyester, nylon, and rayon are generally colorfast (meaning it doesn't bleed), wrinkle-resistant, and durable, making them easy to care for, but they can't handle high heat so keep the dryer on low. Blended fabrics combine the best of both worlds, like cotton/polyester or wool/nylon, and would generally require balanced care. So as you shop for new clothes, consider how much care they will need.

Knowing if clothes are colorfast is key—no one wants whites turned pink by a rogue red sock. Always **check care labels** for instructions. Next, **sort your laundry** by color (whites, lights, darks) and fabric type. Wash whites separately to avoid color bleeding unless you're sure the colors won't run. Separate heavy items, like towels, from lighter clothes to prevent damage, and wash delicates, such as bras or wool sweaters, on their own or by hand for extra care.

Washing your clothes the right way can prevent disasters and extend their life. Start with the right detergent—use HE detergent for high-efficiency machines and gentle options like Woolite for delicates. **Treat stains promptly** with removers like Shout and wash immediately. Follow these general rules: use warm water for cottons, cool for synthetics, and cold for delicates. The more delicate the fabric, the less heat it needs.

Drying clothes properly is essential for maintaining their shape and longevity. Start by shaking clothes out of the washer to minimize wrinkles. Use **dryer sheets** to reduce static cling, and always **clean the lint trap** for better drying efficiency. Avoid over-drying to prevent shrinkage, and air-dry delicates to keep them looking their best. The **Permanent Press** setting on your dryer is great for synthetics, blends, and wrinkle-prone fabrics—a dependable option for most clothing.

Fold clothes right after drying to prevent wrinkles. If you can't, shake them out and lay them flat until you can fold them. This saves time ironing or steaming later. Speaking of steaming, a **clothes steamer** is an easy and often more practical alternative to ironing. Finally, keep your closet or dresser organized to ensure your clothes stay neat and ready to wear.

To minimize laundry time and loads, aim to wash once a week. Combine whites and lights in one load and darks and synthetics in another, adjusting for colorfastness. Wash towels and bedding every other week, alternating if needed. Rewear outerwear (jackets), air out lightly worn items, and spot clean to reduce unnecessary washing. Use a divided hamper to pre-sort clothes and multitask while doing laundry. Start loads during other chores, set timers to avoid delays, and fold clothes immediately to prevent wrinkles and clutter. This streamlined routine keeps your wardrobe fresh with minimal effort.

HOME SAFETY TIPS: PREVENTING AND HANDLING EMERGENCIES

Keeping your home safe is essential for your peace of mind and avoiding costly disasters. Imagine knowing exactly what to do when a smoke detector starts blaring or how to handle a minor kitchen fire without panicking. That's the level of preparedness we're aiming for. **Fire safety** is a top priority, so start with a fire extinguisher—they're affordable and invaluable and you should have one at home. Remember the PASS method: **P**ull the pin, **A**im at the base of the fire, **S**queeze the handle, and **S**weep side to side. It's a simple technique that could be a lifesaver. And speaking of lifesavers, always have your escape routes planned out. Know how to exit your building safely, and never hesitate to call 911 if things get out of hand. Smoke detectors are another essential tool—make sure they're functioning. Test them monthly and replace batteries at least once a year to keep them in top shape.

Kitchen safety involves handling knives with care and always being cautious around hot surfaces. Grease fires can happen quickly, so remember to smother them with a lid or use baking soda—never water. Proper food handling is important too. Avoid cross-contamination by using separate cutting boards for meat and vegetables, and always store food at the right temperatures.

First aid knowledge is just as vital as fire safety and can make all the difference in an emergency. Start by keeping a well-stocked first aid kit in an accessible spot with essentials like bandages and antiseptic wipes. Be familiar with emergency numbers and know when to call for help. If you need to dial 911, stay calm, provide your location clearly, and explain the situation for effective assistance. Follow the ABCs of First Aid to stabilize the patient: A - Airway (ensure it's clear; remove obstructions if safe to do so), B - Breathing (check and assist with rescue breaths as part of CPR if needed), and C - Circulation (stop bleeding or perform chest compressions if there's no pulse). Remember: Stay calm, call 911, and provide first aid until help arrives.

Electrical safety is another area to focus on. Avoid overloading outlets, unplug appliances if they won't be used for a while, and never handle electrical equipment with wet hands. Prepare for power outages by keeping a flashlight handy, knowing your breaker box's location, and learning to reset breakers. For any electrical issues, always call a professional—don't try to fix it yourself.

Water and gas safety are also key. Know where and how to shut off water and gas valves in case of a leak or emergency. Carbon monoxide detectors are vital for detecting this odorless, deadly gas. Know the symptoms of carbon monoxide poisoning, like headaches and dizziness, and act quickly if an alarm sounds.

Your **home's security** is equally important. Keep doors and windows locked, even when you're home, and know how to secure entry points. Never open the door to strangers without verifying who they are. If your home has an alarm system, understand how to use it confidently. Natural disasters can strike without warning, so know the safest places to take shelter during events like tornadoes or earthquakes. Have an emergency kit ready with essentials like water, an emergency blanket, non-perishable food, a flashlight, and batteries. Basic home maintenance plays a role in safety, too. Identify hazards like frayed cords or leaky faucets early on and report them if needed. Maintain clear walkways, ensuring exits are free from clutter. When using cleaning chemicals, always read labels and ensure proper ventilation to avoid harmful fumes.

BASIC HOME REPAIRS

Having the right tools and knowing some basic home repair skills can save you from unnecessary stress, expense, and (let's be honest) maybe a call to your landlord. Here's a quick rundown of the essential tools and repairs you can easily handle on your own:

Must-Have Tools

1. **Hammer**: For everything from hanging artwork to quick furniture fixes.
2. **Screwdrivers (Flathead and Phillips)**: The MVPs for tightening loose screws, assembling furniture, or fixing appliances.
3. **Adjustable Wrench**: Perfect for plumbing tweaks, like stopping that annoying leaky faucet.
4. **Pliers**: For gripping, bending, or even rescuing your stuck earbuds.
5. **Utility Knife**: Handy for opening packages or trimming materials.
6. **Tape Measure**: So you don't end up with a couch that doesn't fit through the door.
7. **Level**: Keeps your shelves and frames looking pro-level straight.
8. **Duct Tape**: The ultimate fix-it tool for quick, temporary repairs.
9. **Allen Wrenches**: Essential for IKEA adventures and other flat-pack furniture.
10. **Flashlight**: Trust me, you'll thank yourself during a blackout or when peering under the sink.

Quick Fixes You'll Want to Master

- **Tighten Loose Screws**: Wobbly chairs or squeaky hinges? Screwdrivers to the rescue.
- **Unclog a Drain**: With a plunger or drain snake, you'll keep your sink or shower flowing smoothly.
- **Fix a Leaky Faucet**: Tighten connections or swap out a washer—no more drip-drip-drip.
- **Change a Light Bulb**: It's basic but essential. Just pick the right wattage and don't overthink it.

- **Patch Nail Holes**: A little spackle and a putty knife can make walls look brand new.
- **Reset Tripped Breakers**: Learn your way around the breaker box—it's your power's HQ.
- **Stop a Running Toilet**: Jiggling the chain or adjusting the flapper can save gallons of water.
- **Seal Drafty Windows**: Weatherstripping and caulk keep your place cozy (and your energy bill low).
- **Hang Heavy Decor**: With wall anchors and a drill, you can securely hang even your heaviest shelves. But before you start drilling, take a moment to think—avoid drilling into potential electrical wires by using a stud finder with wire detection. Safety first!

These basics are all about making your place feel like home without the drama. And hey, if a repair feels way over your head, call in the pros—because some fixes are better left to the experts!

UNDERSTANDING UTILITIES: MANAGING BILLS AND ENERGY USE

Utilities might not be the most exciting topic, but they're essential to keeping your home running smoothly. Think of **electricity** as the heartbeat of your space, powering everything from lights to your gaming console. **Water** is equally vital, not just for drinking, but for cooking, cleaning, and staying hygienic. **Gas** handles heating and cooking, ensuring warm showers and perfectly cooked meals (though some places may only have electric heating and stoves). And of course, the **internet** and cable keep you connected to the world, informed, entertained, and in touch. And don't forget **garbage and recycling services**—knowing your pickup schedule and local disposal rules keeps your home clean and avoids unnecessary fines. Understanding these utilities and managing them efficiently can save you a ton of headaches and cash.

Reading utility bills can seem confusing at first, but once you understand what to look for, they're pretty simple. Bills break down your usage, the rates you're charged, and the total amount due. They might also compare your current usage to previous months, helping you spot patterns. Pay attention to whether peak hours differ from off-peak hours, as energy rates can vary. To save, try shifting activities like running the dishwasher or doing laundry to off-peak times, like late at night or during weekdays.

Cutting utility costs is all about being smart with your resources. Consider using LED bulbs; they last longer and use a fraction of the energy compared to traditional bulbs. Fix leaky faucets and install low-flow showerheads to prevent gallons of water from being wasted. For heating and cooling, adjusting your thermostat a few degrees warmer in the summer or cooler in the winter can add up to big savings. Even small changes, like using fans to help circulate air, can have a noticeable impact. And when it's time to replace your appliances, switch to energy-efficient appliances, such as Energy Star-rated ones.

Technology can help too. Smart meters allow you to track your consumption in real-time, and apps can provide insights into how to cut back. Regularly check for leaks or inefficiencies in your home and ensure appliances are working properly. Small adjustments can lead to big savings, keeping your home and wallet happy.

ACTION PLAN

1. **Set Up a Cleaning Plan That Fits Your Life:**

   - Choose a daily slot for quick tidying—right after breakfast or before bed works great.

- Create a weekly schedule for bigger tasks like vacuuming, laundry, and taking out the trash.
- Tackle monthly deep-cleaning tasks like wiping inside the fridge, dusting ceiling fans and blinds, or cleaning under furniture.
- Keep it simple and consistent—small, regular efforts prevent overwhelming messes.

2. **Now, let's dive into laundry**:

- Gather your week's laundry and sort laundry by color and fabric type to avoid mishaps.
- Use the correct washer settings (delicates, cold water, etc.) and check care labels if something goes wrong.
- Fold clothes immediately after drying to keep them wrinkle-free—it saves you time ironing later.

3. **Ensure Home Safety**:

- Check that all door and window locks are secure and functioning—repair or report any issues immediately.
- Test smoke detectors and replace batteries regularly.
- Keep a first aid kit and fire extinguisher handy and know how to use it.
- Locate your circuit breaker, gas shut-off, and water main, and learn how to shut them off for emergencies.
- Create an emergency plan—know where to go and what to do in case of fire, flood, or power outages.
- Make an emergency contact list. Include numbers for local emergency services, family, housemates, and your landlord. Save it to your phone and post a copy on your fridge for easy access.

4. **Tackle Basic Repairs**:

- Build your DIY toolkit with the essentials with the essentials: a hammer, screwdrivers (flathead and Phillips), adjustable wrench, pliers, utility knife, duct tape, tape measure, flashlight, and a few nails or screws —check garage sales for affordable finds.
- **Master Quick Fixes**: Learn 1-2 simple repairs like unclogging a drain or patching holes, and practice at home or help a friend or neighbor.

5. **Make Your Home More Efficient and Save Money**:

- Track your energy and water usage—turn off lights when you leave a room and fix leaks to save money.
- Set reminders to pay bills on time to avoid late fees.
- Shop around for providers to ensure you're getting the best rates.

With these steps, you'll maintain a clean, safe space and be ready for emergencies. These skills make life easier and help you build confidence in managing your home.

10

BUYING AND MAINTAINING A CAR

FREEDOM ON WHEELS: WEIGHING THE PROS AND CONS OF CAR OWNERSHIP

Imagine gripping the steering wheel, your favorite playlist blaring, and the open road ahead. Owning a car feels like freedom—no more waiting for buses or begging for rides. But before diving into the excitement, take a moment to weigh the responsibilities. Cars come with costs: fuel, insurance, repairs, and yes, parking tickets. There's also the maze of traffic, parking challenges, and the environmental impact. The independence is tempting, but is it worth it? Consider if public transport or ridesharing might work just as well for your lifestyle.

Still deciding if a car is right for you? Remember, ownership includes maintenance: oil changes, tire rotations, brake checks, and potentially costly repairs if you own an older car. Insurance is essential and often pricey for young drivers, so shop around for the best rates and discounts. Don't overlook the environmental impact either. Cars are convenient but come with a footprint. Weigh your needs, budget, and values. Whether you go for it or stick to alternatives, ensure it's the right choice for you. A car can be a powerful tool for freedom—if you're ready for the responsibility that comes with it.

FINDING YOUR PERFECT RIDE

Buying a car is a bit like finding the right pair of shoes—it needs to fit your lifestyle, your budget, and, of course, your style. Start by thinking about how you'll use the car. Are you zipping around the city and need something compact and fuel-efficient? Or maybe you're planning epic road trips and a larger vehicle with extra cargo space is more your speed? Once you've got an idea, it's time to tackle the **budget**. It's tempting to go all out, but staying grounded is key. Ideally, you should avoid taking out a loan if possible. But if a loan is necessary, try to keep your car expenses, including payments, insurance, and gas, within 15-20% of your monthly income. This way, your car remains a source of freedom, not financial stress.

When choosing between a **new or used** car, remember that new cars come with warranties and tech but lose value fast. Used cars are more affordable but may require more maintenance. To ensure you're getting a **fair price**, check the car's value on resources Kelley Blue Book (KBB), Edmunds, and TrueCar, and compare prices on local listings like Autotrader or Craigslist.

When shopping, don't settle for the first car you see. Test drive several models to compare **comfort, visibility, and handling**. Pay attention to legroom, how it drives on highways and in city traffic, and how it performs in different conditions. **Fuel efficiency** matters too—better gas mileage means fewer trips to the pump and more money in your pocket. Check the MPG (miles per gallon) ratings and consider hybrid or fuel-efficient options if gas costs are a concern. Also, be sure to shop for **insurance** during this process. Car insurance can be a significant part of your monthly car expenses, and costs vary widely depending on the type of car you choose. Sports cars and luxury vehicles typically come with higher premiums, while sedans and economy cars tend to be more affordable to insure. Getting estimates early will help you factor insurance costs into your overall budget before making a decision.

Before buying a used car, get a **vehicle history report** from Carfax or AutoCheck to check if the car's been in any accidents or undergone major repairs. Also, have a trusted mechanic **inspect the car** for hidden issues. This small investment can save you from buying a car that'll drain your wallet with endless repairs.

Armed with all this information, you'll be in a strong position to **negotiate**. If the asking price is higher than what you found through your research, don't hesitate to counter-offer or walk away. You have the power to negotiate for a price that aligns with the car's value and condition. Remember, there are plenty of cars—and deals—out there. Just like in any good negotiation, patience and persistence often pay off in securing the ride that suits both your needs and your wallet.

PAYING FOR YOUR RIDE

If you're torn between **buying a car outright or financing** it (taking out a loan), here's the deal: if you've got enough saved up, buying outright means no debt or interest, and that's a win. But if paying upfront would drain your savings, financing might be the better option—it lets you spread out the payments while keeping some cash for other things. Plus, making regular payments can boost your credit score, which is huge for your financial future. Just keep in mind that financing means paying interest, and cars lose value over time, so it's important to check interest rates and make sure the payments fit your budget. Weigh your options, and go with what gives you the best balance of freedom and financial peace of mind!

If you decide to finance, there are a few different paths you can take when it comes to car loans. Dealer financing might seem convenient since it's all wrapped up in one place but watch out for high interest rates. Bank or credit union loans often offer better rates, making them worth a look. Shop around before shopping for a car, so you know where to get the best loans when you're ready to make an offer.

When you're figuring out what you can afford, online calculators are a lifesaver. A **car loan payment calculator** helps you break down monthly payments based on the loan amount, interest rate, and term length. When choosing a loan term, think about the **36 to 60-month** range. A **36-month term** means faster payments and less interest, but your monthly payments will be higher. If you opt for a **60-month term**, your payments will be lower, but you'll pay more in interest overall. A **48-month term** is a sweet spot with a good balance of payments and interest. Just don't forget to factor in costs like insurance, taxes, maintenance, and gas—those can sneak up on you! The goal is to pick a plan that fits your budget without stretching it too thin, giving you the freedom to pay off the car at a pace that works for you.

If you're financing a car anyway, treat it as a golden opportunity to boost your credit score. Paying your car loan on time shows lenders you're responsible, which can make a big difference when you're looking to rent an apartment or get a credit card. Your credit score is like your financial reputation, so keeping it in good shape is crucial. Think of it as an investment in your future—every on-time payment is a step toward a healthier credit score, unlocking more financial options and better interest rates down the road.

Top Tips for Financing a Car
- **Check Your Credit Score**: Know where you stand before applying for loans.
- **Research Loan Options**: Compare rates from dealers, banks, and credit unions before shopping for a car.
- **Use Online Calculators**: Calculate potential monthly payments, including all costs like insurance, taxes, and maintenance.
- **Stay Within Budget**: Ensure your car expenses fit comfortably into your financial plan.
- **Build Your Credit**: View timely payments as a chance to boost your credit score and open up future financial opportunities.

PROTECTING YOUR INVESTMENT

Now it's time to tackle car insurance. It can seem like a whole new language, but trust me, it's an essential part of owning a car. Think of insurance as your safety net, ready to catch you if life throws a curveball. Car insurance typically covers a few key things: **Liability insurance takes** care of the damage you cause to others if you're at fault in an accident. **Collision insurance** steps in when your car gets banged up, no matter who's at fault. **Comprehensive coverage** steps in for those unpredictable moments like theft, vandalism, or natural disasters. And **uninsured/underinsured motorist coverage** has your back if someone without enough insurance crashes into you. Having these coverages means you're protected in different situations—so you're not left stranded in the aftermath of an accident.

Insurance can be pricey, but there are ways to lighten the load. If you're a good student or have a spotless driving record, you could score some sweet **discounts**. Many insurance companies offer lower rates for people with good grades, those who complete safe driving courses, or even for having a car with advanced safety features. Additionally, if you drive fewer miles each year, you may qualify for a low-mileage discount. And if you can pay your premium in full upfront, some companies offer a pay-in-full discount. These discounts can really reduce your monthly premium, so it's worth asking your provider what you might be eligible for. Plus, the safer the car you drive, the better your rates might be, so keep that in mind when picking your ride!

Don't settle for the first insurance quote you get—shopping around can save you big bucks. Get quotes from a few companies and compare them side by side. It might take some time, but it's totally worth it. Look beyond just the price; check out the coverage each policy offers, plus any extra perks like roadside assistance or rental car reimbursement. These bonuses can give you extra peace of mind without draining your wallet. And if you find a good deal, don't be afraid to negotiate—sometimes just asking can score you an even better rate.

Remember, insurance is more than just a legal must—it's a way to protect yourself and your car. A little time spent comparing your options now could save you a lot in the long run. So, take the time to understand what you're getting, and don't be afraid to ask questions. Your future self will thank you for being smart about it!

KEEPING YOUR RIDE IN TIP-TOP SHAPE

Owning a car is just the start—keeping up with basic maintenance is key to keeping your car running smoothly and avoiding costly surprises.

- **Change the oil** regularly (every 3,000–5,000 miles)
- **Check tire pressure** monthly, and rotate tires - tire rotation moves tires to different positions to ensure even wear - every 6,000–8,000 miles for better gas mileage and longer tire life.
- Pay attention to your **brakes**—squealing or vibrations mean it's time for new pads.
- **Replace the air filter** every 12,000–15,000 miles to boost engine performance and fuel efficiency.
- **Replace wiper blades** yearly, and top off washer fluid for clear visibility.
- **Keep your car clean** inside and out to protect its value.
- **Inspect belts and hoses** for wear. Check essential fluids like coolant, brake, and transmission fluid, and keep your battery terminals clean to avoid starting issues.

Your owner's manual is your guidebook here, laying out a schedule that helps you keep track of when these tasks need doing. Skipping maintenance might feel like a time- or money-saver now, but it usually leads to bigger bills and more stress later. A little effort now means fewer surprises and more peace of mind down the road.

Know Your Warning Lights. Dashboard warning lights might look intimidating, but think of them as your car's way of sending you important texts. If a light pops on, don't ignore it—address it ASAP to avoid bigger headaches later. The **check engine light** may feel like a minor nuisance, but it's actually a heads-up to get your car checked before small issues turn into major ones. The **oil pressure light** is more urgent—it means your oil is dangerously low, so pull over and top it up to avoid wrecking your engine. The **battery light** signals a low charge or electrical issue, so don't wait too long before investigating, or you could end up stuck. And if the **tire pressure light** comes on, it's time to check and inflate your tires. Proper tire pressure improves fuel efficiency and helps your tires last longer. These lights aren't just decorations—they're lifesavers when you pay attention.

Always have an **emergency kit** in your car, ready for the unexpected. Include a spare tire and jack, jumper cables, a flashlight with extra batteries, a first aid kit, and a blanket and water. These essentials can make a big difference in an emergency, whether it's a breakdown or an unexpected wait in bad weather.

Flats happen unexpectedly, and knowing how to change a tire can save you from being stuck on the side of the road. Start by finding a safe spot to pull over and turn on your hazard lights. Use a wrench to loosen the lug nuts, then jack up the car and fully remove them. Swap the flat with a spare tire, tighten the lug nuts, lower the car, and give them a final tighten for good measure. Practice changing a tire at home so you're ready when it matters. Need a visual guide? Check out YouTube for step-by-step instructional videos. It's a straightforward skill, but having it in your back pocket can be a lifesaver.

Fuel Efficiency Hacks and Road Trip Prep. Saving gas isn't just good for your wallet—it's also a win for the planet. Want to save on fuel? Keep it simple: don't speed (driving over 60 mph guzzles gas), make sure your tires are properly inflated, and lighten your car's load by ditching the stuff you don't need. Planning a road trip? Give your car a little love first—check your tire pressure, oil levels, and lights. Pack an emergency kit, load up on snacks, and don't forget to curate an epic playlist to set the vibe. A little prep goes a long way toward keeping your ride smooth and your journey stress-free.

DRIVING RESPONSIBLY

Driving responsibly isn't just about following traffic laws—it's about keeping yourself and others safe. **Stay alert** by checking mirrors, keeping a safe distance, and anticipating other drivers' moves. **Defensive driving** helps you react quickly to sudden changes, making the road safer and your drives less stressful.

Distractions are a major risk. Checking your phone, eating, or even chatting too much with passengers can take your focus off the road. Set your playlist or GPS before driving, and keep your phone out of reach. If you need to text or call, pull over safely first. And it's not just phones—eating, fumbling with the radio, or even chatting with passengers can pull your focus away from driving. Prioritize the road.

Traffic laws exist for a reason—speeding, rolling through stop signs, and running red lights put lives at risk and can significantly raise your insurance rates. A clean driving record saves you money and prevents accidents.

Being a responsible driver also means knowing **when not to drive**. If you're tired, stressed, or have had a drink, it's better to find another way home. Fatigue can be as dangerous as alcohol, slowing your reaction time and impairing judgment. If you're feeling sleepy, take a break, grab a coffee, or switch drivers if you're with someone else. And never underestimate the impact of weather. Rain, snow, or fog can change driving conditions drastically. Slow down, increase your following distance, and use your headlights when visibility is low. These small adjustments can make a big difference in staying safe.

Safe driving is all about smart choices. Stay focused, drive defensively, and respect the road—you'll protect yourself and everyone around you. Plus, it helps you avoid fines and keep your insurance premiums low.

ACTION PLAN

Path 1: If You're Shopping for a Car

1. **Decide If You Need a Car:**
   - Assess your needs vs. wants—could public transport or ridesharing cover your lifestyle while saving money?

2. **Create a Budget:**
   - Factor in car payments, insurance, gas, and maintenance to ensure car ownership fits your finances.

3. **Get Your License:**
   - If you don't already have one, research local licensing requirements and consider a driver's education course.

4. **Shop Smart:**
   - Research new and used cars, compare pros and cons, and calculate total monthly costs to find a car that fits your budget and lifestyle.

Path 2: If You Already Own a Car

1. **Follow Your Owner's Manual Maintenance Schedule:**
   - Stay on top of oil changes, brake checks, and tire care to keep your car running smoothly and efficiently.
   - Be proactive. Regular maintenance prevents costly repairs and ensures your safety on the road.

2. **Inspect Regularly**:
    - Check your car for unusual noises, tire wear, and proper inflation—especially before a road trip.
    - Prepare for a road trip by checking fluid levels (oil, coolant, wiper fluid), testing your lights, and ensuring your tires are road-ready.

3. **Prepare an Emergency Kit**:
    - Stock your car with essentials like a first aid kit, flashlight, jumper cables, basic tools, water, snacks, and a blanket.

4. **Shop Around for Insurance**:
    - Periodically compare insurance providers to ensure you're getting the best rates and coverage.

Car ownership is just one part of adulting. From budgeting to maintenance, each builds skills that help in other areas of life. A car is a tool—manage it wisely, and it becomes a valuable asset. Now that you've got the know-how, you're ready to take on other adult responsibilities with confidence!

YOU'VE GOT THIS!

Congratulations! You've just taken a huge step toward mastering adulthood. Throughout the chapters, we've covered a lot of ground. From managing your finances to whipping up a meal plan, we've tackled the essential skills needed to thrive in adult life. We delved into the basics of financial literacy, helping you transform money from a source of stress into a tool for achieving your dreams. We ventured into renting an apartment and buying a car. And let's not forget about maintaining your health, managing your time, and navigating the world of work and relationships. Each chapter was designed to build your confidence and independence step by step.

What's Next?

Learning doesn't stop here—life will throw unexpected challenges your way, and that's okay. Every experience is an opportunity to grow. Keep asking questions, trying new things, and leveling up your skills. Whether it's budgeting for an apartment or negotiating a raise, each step makes you stronger and more capable.

Confidence in adulting comes from doing. You've got the tools—now put them to work. Set small, manageable goals to build momentum.

Mistakes? They're just part of the process. Every challenge you overcome is proof that you're figuring it out.

Start now. Pick one or two skills from this book—set up a budget, cook a homemade meal, or finally get organized. Each step moves you forward. Celebrate the wins, learn from the missteps, and keep growing.

Your Game Plan for Success

- **Keep Learning.** Whether it's refining your budgeting skills, trying new recipes, or improving your time management, growth never stops.
- **Stay Organized.** Life can get chaotic, but using calendars, to-do lists, and budgeting apps can help keep you on track.
- **Embrace Challenges.** Mistakes will happen, and that's okay. Learn from them and keep moving forward.
- **Prioritize Yourself.** Take care of your mental and physical health so you have the energy to chase your dreams.

Building the Life You Want

The best part about adulthood? You get to design a life that works for you. Whether that means traveling the world, landing your dream job, building wealth, or simply having the independence to make your own choices—it's all within your reach. The skills you've learned here will help you get there.

Adulting isn't about knowing everything—it's about being resourceful, adaptable, and willing to learn. You don't need to have all the answers right away, but you do need the skills to figure things out. Stay curious, keep practicing, and don't be afraid to ask for help when you need it.

So go out there, take charge, and create the life you want. You've got this!

REFERENCES

Financial Literacy: What It Is, and Why It Is So Important To ... https://www.investopedia.com/terms/f/financial-literacy.asp

Best Banks and Credit Unions of 2024 https://www.nerdwallet.com/p/best/banking/best-banks-and-credit-unions

The 50/30/20 Budget Rule Explained https://www.bankrate.com/banking/what-is-the-50-30-20-rule/

The Complete Guide to Understanding Credit Scores https://www.experian.com/blogs/ask-experian/credit-education/score-basics/understanding-credit-scores/

Learning How to Cook: A Guide for Beginners https://www.escoffier.edu/blog/value-of-culinary-education/learning-how-to-cook-a-guide-for-beginners/

Simple Healthy Meal Plan for Young Adults https://healthbeet.org/healthy-meal-plan-young-adults/

17+ College Kitchen Basics You ACTUALLY Need https://thepracticalkitchen.com/college-kitchen-basics/

How to Feed Teens on a Budget - The Scramble https://www.thescramble.com/cooking-eating-on-a-budget/how-to-feed-teens-on-a-budget/

Importance of Good Personal Hygiene for Teenagers - Lesson https://study.com/academy/lesson/importance-of-good-personal-hygiene-for-teenagers.html#:~:text=During%20this%20time%20of%20physical,the%20adoption%20of%20social%20norms.

The Mental Health Benefits of Exercise https://www.helpguide.org/wellness/fitness/the-mental-health-benefits-of-exercise

USDA MyPlate Nutrition Information for Young Adults https://www.myplate.gov/life-stages/young-adults

Screening Tests for Young Adults https://labtestsonline.org.uk/screenings/young-adults

A Student's Guide to the Eisenhower Matrix https://elitepathedu.com/2023/11/16/mastering-productivity-a-students-guide-to-the-eisenhower-matrix/

Pomodoro Technique: History, Steps, Benefits, and ... https://www.verywellmind.com/pomodoro-technique-history-steps-benefits-and-drawbacks-6892111

The Best Task Management Apps for 2024 https://www.pcmag.com/picks/the-best-task-management-apps

10 SMART Goals for College Students in 2024 (with ... https://clickup.com/blog/smart-goals-for-college-students/

Teen Resume Examples & Writing Tips https://resumegenius.com/resume-samples/resume-examples-for-teens

Essential Networking Strategies for Young Professionals to ... https://www.socialmediabutterflyblog.com/2024/04/essential-networking-strategies-for-young-professionals-to-build-lasting-career-connections/

37 First Job Interview Questions (With Example Answers) https://ca.indeed.com/career-advice/interviewing/first-job-interview-questions

Workplace Etiquette: 21 Dos and Don'ts https://graduate.northeastern.edu/resources/workplace-etiquette/

How to Budget for Your First Apartment (Checklist and Tips) https://www.apartmentlist.com/renter-life/first-apartment-budgeting-checklist

Understanding Lease Agreements: Key Terms Every Renter ... https://portlandrentalhomes.com/understanding-lease-agreements-key-terms-every-renter-should-know/

The Roommate Agreement: Why You Need One & How to ... https://www.rentcafe.com/blog/apartmentliving/roommates/roommate-agreement-2/

How to Be a Good Tenant https://www.hgtv.com/lifestyle/real-estate/how-to-be-a-good-tenant

Easy & Effective House Cleaning Tips for Teens https://serenityclean.com/easy-and-effective-house-cleaning-tips-for-teens-boosting-tidiness-effortlessly/

How to separate laundry and sort clothes https://tide.com/en-us/how-to-wash-clothes/how-to-do-laundry/how-to-sort-your-laundry-for-the-best-results

6 Home Safety Tips to Teach Kids & Teenagers https://simplyfamilymagazine.com/6-home-safety-tips-to-teach-kids-and-teenagers

How to Read and Reduce Your Utility Bills - UF/IFAS Blogs https://blogs.ifas.ufl.edu/sarasotaco/2024/03/25/understanding-your-utilities-how-to-read-and-reduce-your-utility-bills/

Communication Skills for Teens: 7 Skills Every Teen ... https://www.daniel-wong.com/2024/04/08/communication-skills-for-teens/

18 Relationship Building Activities, Games, & Ideas for ... https://teambuilding.com/blog/relationship-building

Youth Conflict Resolution Techniques + Life Skills https://elcentronc.org/advocacy/youth-conflict-resolution-techniques-life-skills-processing-conflict-during-a-crisis/

Social Etiquette: 50+ Rules for Everyone to Follow https://www.wikihow.com/Social-Etiquette

Social Media Reputation Management: An A-Z Guide https://www.sprinklr.com/cxm/social-media-reputation-management/

How To Properly Set Up Your Social Media Privacy Settings https://www.aura.com/learn/social-media-privacy-settings

How to Recognize and Avoid Phishing Scams https://consumer.ftc.gov/articles/how-recognize-and-avoid-phishing-scams

Top 20 Social Networking Etiquette Tips for Teens https://www.psychologytoday.com/us/blog/teen-angst/201512/top-20-social-networking-etiquette-tips-teens

Best First Cars for Teens and New Drivers in 2024, Tested https://www.caranddriver.com/rankings/best-cars-for-teens

How to Negotiate a New-Car Price Effectively https://www.consumerreports.org/cars/car-pricing-negotiation/how-to-negotiate-a-new-car-price-effectively-a8596856299/

Basic Car Maintenance Tips & Services Checklist https://www.toyota.com/car-tips/basic-car-maintenance-tips-services-checklist/

Car Insurance for Teens and New Drivers https://www.statefarm.com/insurance/auto/car-insurance-for-teens

Help the Next Young Adult Succeed

Life is easier when we **share what we know**. Now that you've picked up skills to **manage money, cook meals, land a job, and navigate life with confidence**, why not **help someone else do the same**?

Leaving a **quick, honest review on Amazon** helps other young adults find the same **practical advice, confidence, and real-world skills** that made a difference for you.

Your review could be the reason someone finally:

- ✅ **Learns how to budget** and stops running out of money too soon.
- ✅ **Aces their first job interview** and lands a job they actually like.
- ✅ **Stops relying on instant ramen** and figures out how to cook real meals.
- ✅ **Feels more in control** instead of overwhelmed by responsibilities.

Pass It On!

It takes **less than a minute** and costs nothing, but your review could **help someone else feel ready to take on life**.

👉 **Click here to leave your review:**

[https://www.amazon.com/review/review-your-purchases/?asin=BOOKASIN]

Thanks for being part of this journey. **Your words could be exactly what someone else needs to see!**

www.ingramcontent.com/pod-product-compliance
Lightning Source LLC
LaVergne TN
LVHW051950060526
838201LV00059B/3587